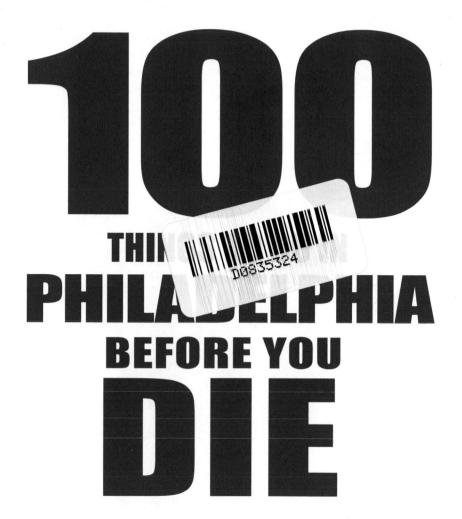

100

THINGS TO DO IN

PHILADELPHIA

BEFORE YOU

DIE

One Liberty Observation Deck
Photo Credit: Steve Belkowitz

100

THINGS TO DO IN
PHILADELPHIA
BEFORE YOU
DIE

• •

IRENE LEVY BAKER

REEDY PRESS

Library of Congress Control Number: 2016936115

ISBN: 9781681060415

Design by Jill Halpin

Cover Image: Avenue of the Arts. Photo Credit: BLKphoto.com for PHLCVB.

Printed in the United States of America
16 17 18 19 20   5 4 3 2

Please note that websites, phone numbers, addresses, and company names are subject to change or cancellation. We did our best to relay the most accurate information available, but due to circumstances beyond our control, please do not hold us liable for misinformation. When exploring new destinations, please do your homework before you go.

DEDICATION

I would like to thank my family for their enthusiasm and support.

CONTENTS

• •

Music and Entertainment

• •

Sports and Recreation

● ●

• •

Shopping and Fashion

● ●

PREFACE

The hardest part of writing this book was limiting the list of "things to do" in Philadelphia to only 100. I had to be very cut-throat in choosing only the very best so readers would get a well-curated list of how to spend their time in Philadelphia. The book includes the city's most popular attractions as well as little-known gems that will be new to even lifelong Philadelphians. Plus tips on getting the most out of each experience—whether it's how to score reservations at the hottest new restaurants or how to make your apathetic teen's jaw drop or where to keep your toddler busy on a rainy afternoon.

I moved to Philadelphia in 1991. In my role at the Philadelphia Convention and Visitors Bureau, I gave tours to travel writers, who are notoriously hard to impress. I noted what surprised and delighted them. Then I opened my firm, Spotlight Public Relations, and my family became my guinea pigs. I took my children to shows and exhibits, my out-of-town visitors to restaurants and museums, and my husband to anything I thought would convince him that we should move from the suburbs to the city.

In the process, I fell in love with Philadelphia. My goal with this book is to inspire you to fall in love with the city too.

This book would not have been possible without the enthusiasm and support of David Baker, Adam and Rachel Baker, Sharon and Marvin Levy, David Levy, June, Dan and Jill Baker,

Karoline Adler, Karol Appel, Bruce and Ellen Asam, Cari Feiler Bender, Brittany Benjamin, Sandy Capps, Steven Cobb, Jeff Cohen, Julie Cohen, David De Silva, Greg DeShields, Natalie Dyen, Khaila Edward Burke-Green, Michelle Eisenberg, Sally Eisenberg, Rachel Ezekiel-Fishbein, Martha Falcon, Rhenda Fearrington, Joel Fishbein, Ellen Friedman, Linda George, Alicia Granor, Neil Greenberg, Cheryl Giusti, Raj "LushLife" Haldar, Bill Hyman, Councilman Kenyatta Johnson, Karin Kaplan, Eric Keiles, Michael Klein, Ellen Kornfield, Stacey Lopez, Jill Magerman, Ellen Matz, Christopher Mullins, Jr., Larry Needle, Robin and Ron Neifeld, Ilene Schafer, Meryl Silver, Ellen Steinbrink Soloff, Jennifer Streitwieser, Janice Telstar, Alex Tewfik, and Deirdre Wright. Thanks also to the staffs at the Philadelphia Convention and Visitors Bureau, Visit Philadelphia, the many attractions listed in this book, as well as the folks at Reedy Press; and fellow authors, especially Judy Colbert, Beth Geisler, and Jeremy Pugh, who shared their expertise and ideas.

Want to hear about Philadelphia's upcoming events, new restaurants, and deals on admissions? Have a question or suggestion? Join the discussion on Facebook at www.facebook.com/100ThingsToDoInPhiladelphia, on Twitter @100Philly, and on Instagram @100ThingsToDoInPhiladelphia.

—Irene

• •

FOOD AND DRINK

GET COOKING
AT COOK

Foodies will adore Cook, a sixteen-seat state-of-the-art demonstration kitchen and classroom near Rittenhouse Square. This intimate class setting is the brainchild of restaurateur Audrey Claire, whose two restaurants, an eponymous eatery and Twenty Manning, are located just down the street. Cook offers demonstration-style cooking classes with the city's A-list chefs, as well as knife and butchering skills, a cookbook author series, mixology, and more. You get dinner and a show as well as a chance for one-on-one time with some of Philadelphia's, and the country's, best chefs. About twenty-five classes are offered monthly, and they typically sell out within minutes.

253 S. 20th Street (Rittenhouse Square)
215-735-2665
audreyclairecook.com

TIP
To book a class, sign up for the e-newsletter on the website. You'll get a missive telling you what day and time the monthly class list will be distributed. Be sitting at your computer at that day and time and purchase tickets immediately.

TASTE THE WORLD'S BEST
GELATO (LITERALLY!)

National Geographic called Capogiro Gelato Artisans the No. 1 ice cream spot in the world. It specifically cited the Madagascar Bourbon Vanilla, Saigon Cinnamon, and Thai Coconut Milk, as well as flavors featuring pomegranate, hazelnut, and pumpkin. The *New York Times* raved about the Sea Salt gelato. Stephanie Reitano, who owns the gelateria with her Italian-born husband, John, makes the gelato daily in small batches using seasonal ingredients and creates hard-to-resist displays. The gelateria has created more than four hundred flavors and offers a rotating list of about thirty at a time, so while you may not be able to get these flavors, it's impossible to go wrong at Capogiro.

119 S. 13th Street (Midtown Village), 215-351-0900
117 S. 20th Street (Rittenhouse Square), 215-636-9250
3925 Walnut Street (University City), 215-222-0252
1625 E. Passyunk (South Philly), 215-462-3790
Capofitto Pizzaria & Gelateria, 233 Chestnut Street (Old City), 215-897-9999
capogirogelato.com

TIP
This may be the best tip in the book. According to Capogiro, gelato has half the fat and half the calories of ice cream.

VISIT CHEESE HEAVEN
AT DI BRUNO BROS.

Brothers Danny and Joe Di Bruno immigrated from Italy in the 1930s expecting to find streets paved with gold. Instead they found the cobblestone streets of Philadelphia's Italian Market (9th Street from Wharton to Fitzwater) in South Philly. The brothers, who only had a third grade education but were highly motivated, opened a grocery store that soon evolved into a cheese shop. But Di Bruno Bros. is not just any cheese shop—it's like cheese heaven. Thousands of pounds of imported cheese, as well as cured meats, hang from the ceiling. The tiny seven-hundred-square-foot store is also packed with wooden barrels of olives and shelves of olive oils and gourmet food.

Their grandsons took over in 1998 and added four more locations and an online store. The Rittenhouse Square, Washington Square, Comcast Center, and Ardmore Farmers Market locations have the same amazing selection in a more updated atmosphere.

930 S. 9th Street (East Passyunk)
215-922-2876
dibruno.com

TIP
The cheesemongers are happy to give advice and samples.

Danny and Joe Di Bruno
Photo Credit: Di Bruno Bros.

EAT, SHOP, AND EXPLORE
CHINATOWN

Chinatown, a bustling neighborhood that borders Reading Terminal Market and the Pennsylvania Convention Center, is home to Hong Kongian, Cantonese, Fujianese, Northern Sichuan, and Taiwanese people, restaurants, markets, shops, and businesses, plus a dash of Koreans, Thais, Malaysians, Burmese, and Vietnamese.

Visit the colorful Friendship Gate at 10th and Arch Streets, which was erected in 1984 to commemorate Philadelphia's relationship with sister city Tianjin. It weighs about eighty-eight tons and stands forty feet tall. To really experience Chinatown, don't be shy about wandering into shops, as you'll find unusual souvenirs like teapots, Hello Kitty gear, mah-jongg sets, and great bargains, and plan to have *at least* one meal here.

Philadelphia Chinatown
Vine to Arch Streets, 8th to 11th Streets

Chef Joseph Poon's Wok 'N Walk Tour of Chinatown
215-928-9333
josephpoon.com

TIP
Take Chef Joseph Poon's amazing and amusing Wok 'N Walk Tour of Chinatown. Tours vary but usually include stops at a fortune cookie factory, Chinese herbal medicine store, Chinese bakery, and Asian supermarket, as well as a meal (for groups).

DON'T GET KICKED OUT
OF HOP SING LAUNDROMAT

This mysterious Chinatown speakeasy opened by Lê, a one-named proprietor, has earned lots of kudos, including being called "one of the best bars in the world" by *Conde Nast Traveler*. The elegant bar serves inventive cocktails made with high-end liquors and freshly extracted juices.

The bar is hard to find. It doesn't have a sign, just an iron gate and doorbell. If you do find it, there's no guarantee you'll get in, or stay in. Sneakers and baseball caps will get you turned away. And if you pull out your phone to take a photo, you'll be thrown out. I've seen it happen. Of course, "getting thrown out of Hop Sing Laundromat" has become a badge of honor, as has taking selfies in the bathroom. But if you say you heard that here, I'll deny it.

1029 Race Street (Chinatown)
hopsinglaundromat.com

TIP
Look sharp. Several dozen people get turned away each night for sins such as wearing flip-flops, shorts, caps, and sneakers.

TRY NOT TO LICK
THE BUDINO JAR

The best non-gelato dessert in Philadelphia can be found at Barbuzzo, a trendy restaurant in trendy Midtown Village owned by serial entrepreneurs Marcie Turney and Valerie Safran. In addition to Barbuzzo, the prolific restaurateurs rule the neighborhood with Lolita, Jamonera, Little Nonna's, and their newest, Bud & Marilyn's, as well as shops Grocery, Open House, and Verde, where they sell Marcie Blaine chocolate.

The budino is salted caramel pudding with a dark chocolate crust, vanilla bean caramel, and sea salt served in a half mason jar. The heavenly dessert, which is eaten with a spoon, is a jar-licking marvel of flavor and texture.

110 S. 13th Street (Midtown Village)
215-546-9300
barbuzzo.com

TIP
The chef's counter at Barbuzzo is available to walk-ins on a first-come, first-served basis and provides a nice show while you savor your dessert. If there are no seats available, budinos are also available to go.

Budino at Barbuzzo
Photo Credit: Jason Varney

SAMPLE PHILADELPHIA'S
RESTAURANT SCENE

If you're a local or miraculously planned your visit to the city during Philadelphia Restaurant Week, consider yourself lucky. During this twice-yearly event, more than one hundred restaurants offer special three-course, price fixed lunch and dinner menus. Some restaurants only offer the three-course menu but others also serve items from their *à la carte* menu. It's the ideal time to try the city's vibrant restaurant scene at a discount. Restaurant Week typically lasts twelve days and officially skips Saturdays, though many restaurants offer their event menu every day. Many restaurants sell out during Restaurant Week, so be sure to make reservations. The event, which is pulled together by Center City District, is more than a decade old and was a precursor to similar events held throughout the country.

Throughout Philadelphia
215-440-5500
centercityphila.org

TIP
For great drink and appetizer deals, don't miss Center City Sips, on Wednesdays from 5 to 7 p.m. throughout the summer.

EAT AND SHOP
AT READING TERMINAL MARKET

If this book was titled *One Thing to Do in Philadelphia Before You Die,* visiting Reading Terminal Market, one of the nation's oldest continuously operating farmers' markets, would be a strong contender for the subject. The one hundred-plus-year-old market is a favorite of chefs, locals, tourists, and conventioneers coming from the attached Pennsylvania Convention Center. They come for meat, poultry, seafood, and produce, as well as flowers, cookbooks, crafts, cleverly shaped chocolates, and prepared foods from dozens of family-run food stands. Think gyros thick with freshly carved lamb, Southern fried chicken, cookies stuffed with chips, and other goodies. Find merchants from Lancaster selling their produce and traditional Pennsylvania Dutch foods, except Sundays.

12th & Market Streets (Convention Center District)
215-922-2317
readingterminalmarket.org

TIP
It tends to get busy during lunch hour, especially when there's a big convention in town. Be prepared to be jostled by the crowds or visit on a weekend morning when it's a little quieter.

HAVE A BEER
AT PHILLY'S OLDEST TAVERN

The beer taps at McGillin's Olde Ale House have been flowing since 1860—when Lincoln was elected president and shortly after the Liberty Bell cracked. It's the oldest continuously operating tavern in Philadelphia and one of the oldest in the country. The focus is on homemade comfort food (including a free bowl of soup with every lunch) and regional craft beers (including three house beers made by Stoudt's Brewing in Adamstown, Pennsylvania).

The historic tavern was opened by Pa and Ma McGillin, Irish immigrants who raised their thirteen children upstairs. One of those children sold the bar to Henry Spaniak and his brother in 1958. Henry's daughter, son-in-law, and grandson still run the pub today.

1310 Drury Street (Midtown Village)
215-735-5562
mcgillins.com

TIP
The crowd gets younger as the night gets older. For a quiet visit, go for lunch, go early in the week, or early in the evening. For a younger vibe, visit at night and have a few pitchers with locals and tourists.

McGillin's Olde Ale House
Photo Credit: Thomas Robert Clarke

TAKE A COFFEE BREAK
AT LA COLOMBE

Founders Todd Carmichael and JP Iberti believed America deserved better coffee, so they gave it to us. For twenty years, they've been sourcing and roasting with care, combining ancient and modern coffee traditions from around the world. And the best part is, La Colombe beans are not only good, but they're also responsibly gathered. And in more good news, the coffee company will open approximately one hundred cafes in major cities in the next five years. La Colombe roasts four million pounds of coffee a year—that's 276 million cups of coffee—and just introduced the draft latte, which is cold-brewed coffee and frothed milk, straight from the tap. La Colombe is so good that it's almost always full, despite the fact that it doesn't have Wi-Fi, since it likes to promote a social, lively atmosphere.

130 S. 19th Street (Rittenhouse Square), 215-563-0860
1414 S. Penn Square (Business District), 215-977-7770
1335 Frankford Avenue (Fishtown), 267-479-1600
100 S. Independence Mall West (Historic District), 267-479-1650
915 W. Lancaster Avenue (Bryn Mawr), 215-398-3091
lacolombe.com

Ritz-Carlton, Philadelphia
(Avenue of the Arts)
10 Avenue of the Arts
215-523-8000
ritzcarlton.com

Gran Caffe L'Aquila
(Rittenhouse Square)
1716 Chestnut Street
215-568-5600
grancaffelaquila.com

TIP

After visiting the Christmas Light Show at Macy's or the Pennsylvania Ballet's *Nutcracker*, enjoy thick, rich hot chocolate at the Ritz-Carlton, Philadelphia. This decadent seasonal treat is accompanied by a wooden box that is filled with house-made marshmallows, fresh whipped cream, and shot-glass-sized portions of chopped peppermint, graham crackers, white and dark chocolate curls, sprinkles, and more. Or sip the classic Perugia hot chocolate made with 70 percent dark chocolate at quirky Gran Caffe L'Aquila. It tastes like the love child of hot cocoa and chocolate pudding, and you can add all-natural caramel, vanilla, hazelnut, mint, or "stronger" flavors.

GO FOR THE GOLD
AT ZAHAV

Michael Solomonov, chef-owner of Zahav, was born in Israel, grew up in Pittsburgh, and then, as a teen, returned to Israel. His personal journey eventually brought him to Philadelphia, where he opened Zahav, which is Hebrew for "gold." His modern Israeli cuisine has earned acclaim in *Esquire, Travel + Leisure,* and *Bon Appetit,* and he earned a Best Chef Mid-Atlantic Award from the James Beard Foundation. The restaurant is billed as modern Israeli cuisine, and it incorporates the many cultures that influenced Israeli cooking—eastern European, North African, and Persian. Order like an Israeli and start with the salatim, a daily selection of salads.

Since Zahav, Solomonov and partner Michael Cook have gone on to open other notable Philadelphia restaurants, including Percy Street BBQ and Abe Fisher, featuring foods of the American Jewish experience, as well as Federal Donuts.

237 St. James Place (Society Hill)
215-625-8800
zahavrestaurant.com

TIP
Also worthwhile is the duo's casual hummusiya, Dizengoff, a tiny space offering a variety of hummus, fresh pita, and Middle Eastern salads.

GO FOR THE CHICKEN
AND STAY FOR THE DONUTS

If the words "gourmet" and "fried chicken" don't seem as if they belong in the same sentence, then you've never been to Federal Donuts. Chef Michael Solomonov and business partner Michael Cook, who call themselves CookNSolo, serve Korean-style fried chicken seasoned with coconut curry, buttermilk ranch, or za'atar, a blend of Middle Eastern herbs..

Each chicken order comes with a honey donut but one is never enough. Get more donuts in flavors like strawberry lavender, mint chocolate cookie, and maple bacon and you'll see why the unassuming store fronts often have lines out the door.

1219 S. 2nd Street (South Philly), 267-687-8258
1632 Sansom Street (Rittenhouse Square), 215-665-1101
3428 Sansom Street (West Philly), 267-275-8489
701 N. 7th Street (North Philly), 267-928-3893
federaldonuts.com

TIP
Federal Donuts also has seasonal locations at Citizens Bank Park (section 140) and Spruce Street Harbor Park.

GAIN NEW RESPECT
FOR VEGETABLES

Even if you think you don't like vegetarian restaurants, try Vedge, which uses no animal products in the kitchen. While Chef Rich Landau doesn't eat animal products for ethical reasons, he likes the taste of meat and reportedly creates dishes with a carnivore's palate, like wood roasted carrot kimchee "reuben," with pumpernickel and sauerkraut puree. There's a reason *Travel + Leisure* and *Food & Wine* named it one of the best vegetarian restaurants in the United States, and *GQ* and others call it one of the best in the country (vegetarian or not).

The husband-and-wife-owned restaurant is also known for its innovative cocktails featuring house-made syrups and bitters. It's set in a charming mansion. If you prefer a more casual atmosphere, check out its younger sibling, V Street. Better yet, try both.

Vedge (Washington Square West)	V Street (Rittenhouse Square)
1221 Locust Street	126 S. 19th Street
215-320-7500	215-278-7943
vedgerestaurant.com	vstreetfood.com

TIP
It can be hard to get a reservation between 5:45 and 9 p.m., but the restaurant holds a few tables aside for walk-ins.

AWAKEN YOUR SENSES
AT THE ITALIAN MARKET

In 1884, Antonio Palumbo opened a boarding house for fellow Italian immigrants and a few businesses cropped up in the neighborhood. Soon the area was transformed into one of the country's largest outdoor markets. The tiny shops are stocked to the ceiling with spices, fresh pasta, meat and fish, produce, and baked goods, and their sights and smells spill out onto the sidewalk. Business is conducted right there in front of shoppers, giving the street a bustling old-school feel. And now there are foods and groceries from, and for, new waves of immigrants—including Mexicans, Koreans, and Vietnamese.

The market is open daily, year-round, though it's quieter on Mondays. Wander on your own or take a guided tour.

South 9th Street Italian Market
(East Passyunk)
South 9th Street between Wharton
& Fitzwater
215-278-2903
italianmarketphilly.org

Italian Market Immersion
by Philadelphia Urban Adventures
(East Passyunk)
215-280-3746
www.phillytourhub.com

Taste4Travel Tour (East Passyunk)
610-506-6120
taste4travel.net

TIP
Stop at nearby East Passyunk's restaurant row, where you'll find lots of hip chef-driven restaurants and shops.

● ●

TOAST PHILADELPHIA'S
BEER GARDENS

One reason Philadelphia regularly makes national lists of Best Beer Cities is its awesome seasonal beer gardens, including new beer gardens that pop up around the city every summer, thanks to the Pennsylvania Horticultural Society's successful movement to turn underused lots into imaginative, inviting spaces.

Independence Beer Garden, overlooking Independence National Historical Park, features forty regional and domestic craft beers on tap at multiple bars. Adirondack chairs, picnic tables, ping-pong, and other games lit by twinkling lights make the twenty-thousand-square-foot area feel surprisingly intimate.

If there is heaven on earth, it is Spruce Street Harbor Park, which sits alongside the Delaware River. You'll find locals and tourists enjoying its striped hammocks strung beneath hundreds of color-changing lights, floating food and drink barges transformed into an oasis, cozy seating areas, and oversized games. It's obvious why the *Huffington Post* called it "one of the best urban beaches in the world."

Independence Beer Garden
(Historic District)
100 S. Independence Mall West
215-922-7100
phlbeergarden.com

Spruce Street Harbor Park
(Penn's Landing)
Spruce Street & S. Columbus
Boulevard
215-922-2386
sprucestreetharborpark.com

Spruce Street Harbor Park
Photo Credit: Matt Stanley

EAT LIKE A PHILADELPHIAN—
PRETZELS AND WATER ICE

The average American eats one and a half to two pounds of pretzels a year. Philadelphians eat twelve times that amount. Thanks to the Pennsylvania Dutch, these "little rewards" are available from food carts and street vendors throughout the city. At Miller's Twist in Reading Terminal Market, you can watch pretzels being hand-rolled and then taste them while they're hot and chewy.

It's unclear who invented water ice, but it's widely believed that it arrived in Philadelphia with the wave of Italian immigrants in the late nineteenth and early twentieth centuries. Water ice, aka Italian ice, is a cross between a snow cone, slushie, and chopped popsicle. You'll find it throughout the city, including at Pop's, which is more than eight decades old.

Miller's Twist
(Convention Center District)
Reading Terminal Market
51 N. 12th Street
215-923-1723
millerstwist.com

Pop's Water Ice (East Passyunk)
1337 Oregon Avenue
215-551-7677
popsice.com

TIP
If you want to sound like a Philadelphian, say "wooder ice," not water ice.

ORDER YOUR PHILADELPHIA
CHEESESTEAK WHIZ WIT

Philadelphia is nearly synonymous with cheesesteaks. It's a mouthful, as is Philadelphia's iconic sandwich. The classic place to get a cheesesteak is the corner of 9th and East Passyunk in Philadelphia's Italian Market, where you'll find Pat's King of Steaks catty-corner from Geno's Steaks. Order your cheesesteak "whiz wit" to indicate that you want Cheez Whiz and onions atop your thinly sliced steak on an Amoroso roll. Do *not* be seduced by the provolone or chicken. Go with a friend and get a cheesesteak at each place, then swap halves so you can choose your favorite. No rush, both booths are open twenty-four hours, and nearly every Philadelphian has a story about seeing a limo pull up with a celeb in the wee hours of the morning. Every local has a favorite cheesesteak place. Jim's Steaks and Tony Luke's are also popular.

Pat's King of Steaks (East Passyunk)　　Geno's Steaks (East Passyunk)
1237 E. Passyunk　　　　　　　　　　1219 E. 9th Street
215-468-1546　　　　　　　　　　　　215-389-0659
patskingofsteaks.com　　　　　　　　　genosteaks.com

TIP
These babies are juicy. Eat like a local—
standing up and leaning forward.

TASTE WHAT'S BREWING
IN PHILADELPHIA

During colonial times, it was considered safer to drink beer than water. Today, it's just considered more fun, especially in Philadelphia, which has a wealth of breweries and brewpubs. In the early twentieth century, the region boasted nearly two hundred breweries, but most didn't survive Prohibition. Fortunately, the 1980s brought a new brewery boom.

The region is home to larger microbreweries that offer tours, including Victory, Yards, Flying Fish, and Philadelphia Brewing Company. Also try smaller brewers with tours and brewpubs, like Saint Benjamin, Forest & Main, Round Guys, and Tired Hands with its "brew cafe."

The city even has a week in June devoted to beer—appropriately called Philly Beer Week. The much-copied event includes hundreds of festivals, beer dinners, tours, crawls, tastings, and meet-the-brewer events.

TIP
Have a ball tasting local brews on your own or take a beer tour.

Brewery and Bar Tours

Liberty Brew Tours
267-606-7403
libertybrewtours.com

Philly Brew Tours
215-866-2337
phillybrewtours.com

Philly on Tap by Philadelphia Urban Adventures
215-280-3746
philadelphiaurbanadventures.com

Pub Crawl by Big Red Pedal Tours
215-625-2509
bigredpedaltours.com

Philly Beer Week
phillybeerweek.org

GET THE SCOOP
ON THE BEST ICE CREAM PARLOR

Since the Berley brothers opened Franklin Fountain near Philadelphia's historic attractions in 2004, no one has been able to lick it. *Food & Wine* called it one of the best soda fountains in the country, citing its devotion to history that permeates everything from the antique marble fountain to the copper pots to the vintage ice cream flavors to the period-appropriate mustaches sported by the brothers.

Visit this old-fashioned soda fountain for authentic phosphate sodas, handmade ice cream in flavors ranging from Franklin mint chip to teaberry gum, and the Mt. Vesuvius sundae, which the Food Network called one of the top five ice creams in America.

116 Market Street (Old City)
215-627-1899
franklinfountain.com

TIP
You get to choose your own flavors for what *USA Today* calls the best milkshake in the country. Try peanut butter and black raspberry ice cream together for a mouthful of PB&J goodness.

Franklin Fountain
Photo Credit: Vicki Liantonio

TRY BIG TASTES
AT A TINY RESTAURANT

In 1998, Chef Marc Vetri and partner Jeff Benjamin opened Vetri Ristorante in a tiny townhouse on Spruce Street. Since then, they've earned national recognition and have opened Osteria, Amis, Alla Spina, Lo Spiedo, and multiple Pizzeria Vetri locations. The group joined forces with URBN Inc. in late 2015.

Vetri, an intimate gem with just nine much-sought-after tables, serves tasting menus only. Signature dishes include spinach gnocchi with brown butter and sweet onion crepe with white truffle. Additionally, the restaurant has a 2,500-bottle, Italian-focused wine list.

1312 Spruce Street (Washington Square West)
215-732-3478
vetriristorante.com

TIP
With only thirty seats, it can be tough to snag a reservation. Be flexible about date and time. You can also ask to be added to the waiting list in case there is a cancellation.

BRING YOUR OWN BOTTLE
TO A RESTAURANT

Due to Pennsylvania's Quaker background and its archaic liquor laws, it can be difficult for restaurants to get, or afford, a liquor license. Philadelphia restaurateurs turned lemons into limoncello by opening BYOB—bring your own bottle—establishments. The trend energized the city's restaurant scene and spawned small chef-driven restaurants, mom-and-pop shops, and ethnic restaurants where you can bring your own wine, beer, or spirits. Diners have a wider variety of restaurants to choose from, and by bringing their own booze, they save money since there's no markup on their liquor. A few restaurants charge a corking fee. Most do not. Some are cash only, so be sure to call or check their websites. And many are tiny, so reservations are a good idea.

TIP
Visitors can get wine and spirits at liquor stores.
Beer must be purchased separately at beer distributors.
Some convenience stores sell beer by the bottle or six-pack.

MEET TOP CHEFS
WHO CHOPPED THEIR WAY TO FAME

Philadelphia is a great restaurant city, and the top places tend to fill up quickly. There's no shortage of restaurants by chefs who have chopped their way to fame on Food Network competitions and other cooking shows. *Top Chef* winner Kevin Sbraga serves toothsome four-course prix fixes at Sbraga, and Nick Elmi, another winner, opened a little gem called Laurel on East Passyunk, Philadelphia's hip restaurant row. You'll want to try Iron Chef Jose Garces's reliably good mini-empire including Amada, Tinto, and Village Whiskey and Masaharu Morimoto's namesake restaurant, which is co-owned by prolific restaurateur Stephen Starr. Starr owns nearly two dozen restaurants in the city, including standouts Parc, Serpico, and Talula's Garden. And stop at Carlo's Bakery to find out what's cooking with Cake Boss Buddy Valastro.

TIP
If you can't get a reservation, follow the restaurant/chef on social media. When they get a last-minute cancellation, they often turn to Twitter or Facebook to fill the table.

Sbraga (Avenue of the Arts)
521 S. Broad Street
215-735-1913
sbragadining.com

Laurel (East Passyunk)
1617 E. Passyunk
215-271-8299
restaurantlaurel.com

Morimoto (Historic District)
723 Chestnut Street
215-413-9070
morimotorestaurant.com

Carlo's Bakery (Rittenhouse Square)
2101 Walnut Street
215-309-2033
carlosbakery.com

Restaurant Groups

Garces Group
Amada, Tinto, Village Whiskey, and more
garcesgroup.com

Starr Restaurants
Parc, Serpico, Talula's Garden, and more
starr-restaurant.com

KEEP ON TRUCKIN'
FOR GREAT FOOD

Philadelphia has a booming food truck culture featuring hundreds of trucks with big tastes. Some are casual, while others are surprisingly gourmet. You'll find enthusiastic lines for battered fried cheese curds from the Cow and the Curd, tofu bánh mi waffles from Foolish Waffles, and pumpkin pierogies from Mom-Mom's Polish Food Cart. Other standouts are pork belly slow roasted then served on a bed of Napa cabbage and topped with pickled red onions and truck-made aioli at the Whirly Pig and Cap'n Crunch tilapia burritos at Cucina Zapata. The Revolution Taco truck, Spot Gourmet Burger food cart, and MacMart truck developed such followings that they were each able to open a brick-and-mortar location too.

Revolution Taco
(Rittenhouse Square)
2015 Walnut Street
267-639-5681
therevolutiontaco.com

Spot Gourmet Burger
(Brewerytown)
2821 West Girard Avenue
484-620-6901

MacMart (Rittenhouse Square)
104 S. 18th Street
215-444-6144
macmartcart.com

Street Food for Thought Tour
215-280-3746
phillytourhub.com

TIP
The Street Food for Thought Tour by Philadelphia Urban Adventures combines the fun of street food with brain food on a tour of two college campuses and three food truck hubs.

Where to Find Food Trucks
Some locations are weekdays or weekends only.
Check before heading out. To find specific trucks,
follow them on social media for location updates.

Love Park (Logan Square)
1501 John F. Kennedy Boulevard

The Porch at Amtrak's 30th Street Station (West Philly)
2955 Market Street

Eakins Oval (Logan Square)
2451 Benjamin Franklin Parkway

City Hall
Market & Broad Streets

Drexel University (West Philly)
33rd & Arch

University of Pennsylvania (West Philly)
On Walnut, Chestnut & Spruce from 36th to 38th

Temple University (North Philly)
On 13th, Norris & Montgomery from Broad Street to 12th

City Hall on the Avenue of the Arts.
Photo Credit: bklphoto.com for PHLCVB

MUSIC AND ENTERTAINMENT

FEEL THE ENERGY
ALONG THE AVENUE OF THE ARTS

Broad Street, north and south of City Hall, has been designated the Avenue of the Arts. The vibrant area to the south is the colorfully illuminated home to many of the city's cultural institutions, as well as restaurants and hotels.

The centerpiece is the architecturally stunning Kimmel Center, which houses the Philadelphia Orchestra, the Philly Pops, plus jazz, classical music, theater, and dance performances. The grande dame of the avenue, the Academy of Music, has hosted shows for more than 150 years, including Opera Philadelphia, Pennsylvania Ballet, and the Broadway Philadelphia series. Other neighbors include the Wilma Theater, Suzanne Roberts Theatre, Arts Bank, and Prince Theater. New LED lights stretch two and a half miles along the northern section of Broad Street to the Pennsylvania Academy of the Fine Arts, the Liacouras Center, and New Freedom Theatre.

North & South Broad Street (Avenue of the Arts)
215-731-9668
avenueofthearts.org

TIP
Free one-hour tours of the Kimmel Center are offered daily, and art and architecture tours are offered on Saturdays.

SEE ONE OF THE WORLD'S
HIGHEST-RESOLUTION LED DISPLAYS

Philadelphia had a gentleman's agreement that no building would be taller than the William Penn statue atop City Hall. Liberty Place broke that agreement in 1987 and set off the "curse of Billy Penn," which supposedly caused Philadelphia's sports teams' failure to win championships. The losing streak was broken in 2008, when the Phillies won the World Series—just sixteen months after a statuette of William Penn was affixed at the topping-off ceremony of the Comcast Center, then the tallest building in Pennsylvania. Local sports fans are holding their breath, since the even taller Comcast Innovation and Technology Center will open in 2018.

The Comcast Center's lobby is dominated by a two-thousand-square-foot LED screen, displaying more than ten million pixels, with resolution that's five times higher than HDTV. Incredibly realistic imagery of nature, architecture, and culture, seems to jump off the screen and immerse viewers.

Comcast Center (Center City West)
17th & JFK Boulevard
themarketandshopsatcomcastcenter.com

TIP
Stop at the nicer-than-usual food court downstairs.

STRUT
WITH THE MUMMERS

For many Philadelphians, the real New Year's party isn't on December 31, it's on January 1, when hundreds of thousands gather to watch the Mummers Parade. This colorful, crowded, chaotic, creative cacophony has been going on for more than 115 years, making it the oldest continuous folk parade in the United States. So bundle up and join the fun, which includes seven hours of music, elaborate costumes, and dancing by more than ten thousand participants.

Not in Philadelphia for New Year's Day? You can still get a taste of this iconic Philadelphia tradition by visiting the Mummers Museum. In addition to hearing about the customs of mummers, you'll find displays of elaborate costumes and learn how to do the mummers' strut.

1100 South 2nd Street at Washington Avenue (Pennsport)
215-336-3050
mummersmuseum.com

TIP
If you take a cab, sound like a local by saying "Two Street" instead of Second Street. If you drive, parking in the museum lot is free.

TRAVEL TO THE TOP
OF CITY HALL

It took more than thirty years to build City Hall in the original center of the city. The result is the largest municipal building in the United States, with seven hundred rooms on four and a half acres. It's not only big, but it's also beautiful, adorned with sculptures of allegorical figures, heads, and continents by Alexander Milne Calder. His twenty-seven-ton statue of city founder William Penn atop the tower reaches 548 feet—the world's tallest masonry structure without a steel frame.

Take an elevator to the bottom of the Penn statue for panoramic views of the city. Timed tickets are available at the visitor center. A longer tour is offered once a day for more about the building's history, art, and architecture.

City Hall
Broad & Market Streets
215-686-2840

TIP
Tours fill up fast. Come early in the day for same-day tickets.

TUNE IN
TO VICTOR CAFE

John DiStephano, a young Italian immigrant who loved classical music and grand opera, settled in Philadelphia in 1908 and opened a gramophone shop that served espresso, spumoni, and a steady diet of music. After Prohibition, he purchased a liquor license and his shop became a full-fledged restaurant, which was eventually run by his son and then grandchildren.

Today Victor Cafe provides an unforgettable experience where performers and opera students moonlighting as servers break into song every twenty minutes or so and the walls are lined with signed photos and operatic memorabilia. The menu features Italian classics and wines at reasonable prices.

Victor Cafe, Music Lover's
Rendezvous (East Passyunk)
1303 Dickinson Street
215-468-3040
victorcafe.com

Mario Lanza Museum
(East Passyunk)
712 Montrose
215-238-9691
mariolanzainstitute.org

TIP
Restaurateur John DiStephano, an unofficial scout for RCA, took Alfred Cocozza to the company's headquarters in Camden, New Jersey. Cocozza changed his name to Mario Lanza and became a legendary tenor. While you're in South Philly, make an appointment to tour the kitschy Mario Lanza Institute and Museum, with its collection of memorabilia.

Victor Cafe
Photo Credit: Rachel Baker

VIEW PHILLY
FROM THE TOP

From One Liberty Observation Deck on the fifty-seventh floor of One Liberty Place, you can see all of Philadelphia, over the Ben Franklin Bridge into New Jersey, over the Schuylkill River to West Philadelphia, and well beyond. Interactive touch screens answer your "what is that" and "where is that" questions as you look for a bird's-eye view of your hotel or home. The screens can be translated into French, Spanish, German, or Mandarin. And those chairs aren't only for resting your feet, but also for hearing oral histories of well-known Philadelphians talk pop culture, music, and sports. You'll undoubtedly be inspired to take selfies, and in addition to the views, you can stand by Ben Franklin's feet on the ground floor and his giant bust on the top floor.

1650 Market Street/Liberty Place (Center City West)
215-561-DECK
phillyfromthetop.com

TIP
Plan your trip just before sunset so you can see the daytime view, watch the sun set, and then see the nighttime view too.

PLAY AROUND
AT A THEATRICAL PRODUCTION

While many cultural organizations cluster around Broad Street, creating the Avenue of the Arts, there are more sprinkled throughout the city. Philadelphia has more than twenty professional theater companies that focus on musicals, recent hits, original works, classics, avant garde works, and children's shows. They have helped Philadelphia earn its place on *Travel + Leisure*'s list of most cultured cities.

Choose from crowd pleasers at the Walnut Street Theatre, which opened in 1809, or new works at InterAct Theatre Company, which just moved into a new space. Walnut Street, America's oldest theater, is a National Historic Landmark. InterAct Theatre Company commissions, develops, and produces new plays that explore contemporary social, political, and cultural issues. There are lots of great choices.

Walnut Street Theatre
(Washington Square West)
825 Walnut Street
215-574-3550
walnutstreettheatre.org

InterAct Theatre Company
(Rittenhouse Square)
The Drake, 1512 Spruce Street
215-568-8079
interacttheatre.org

TIP
Walnut Street offers discounts for people under the age of twenty-four, military personnel, and those in the industry, as well as half-priced "day of show" tickets online, by phone, or at the box office.

HEAR A CONCERT
AT WORLD CAFE LIVE

World Cafe Live is a multilevel music venue designed to optimize the live performance experience, and it is the home of WXPN's studio. Everything in the venue is thoughtfully designed—including sight lines, lighting, and acoustics—to make sure patrons have a great experience.

The downstairs hosts live performances by nationally known acts for up to 300 (bistro style) or 650 (standing). Upstairs, there's space for more intimate concerts for 100, and you can get a glimpse of a WXPN broadcast live including the nationally syndicated World Cafe with host David Dye, who intersperses a mix of blues, rock, world, folk, and alternative country music with interviews of well-known and emerging artists. There's food and beverage service throughout the venue.

3025 Walnut Street (West Philly)
215-222-1400
philly.worldcafelive.com

TIP
Don't miss Free at Noon concerts featuring everything from national touring acts to emerging artists nearly every Friday.

EXPERIENCE SOMETHING NEW
AT PAINTED BRIDE ART CENTER

When the Painted Bride opened in 1969, it was part of the alternative movement during which underrepresented artists—women, gays and lesbians, people of color, and the disabled—struggled to gain recognition. This intimate theater and gallery has stayed true to its mission by presenting performances that maximize cultural diversity and visibility in the arts.

Today it stages music, dance, and theater performances and displays work in two art galleries, with a focus on emerging and established local artists. The innovative space has become an internationally lauded arts institution.

230 Vine Street (Old City)
215-925-9914
paintedbride.org

TIP

The stage isn't elevated and there's no reserved seating, except for members. So consider getting a membership (it goes to a good cause) or arriving a little early to get a good seat.

JAZZ IT UP
IN PHILADELPHIA

Down Beat magazine named Chris' Jazz Cafe one of the "100 Great Venues Around the World to Hear Jazz." The intimate lounge/restaurant serving Southern-style cuisine lives up to its billing, with live jazz almost every night. Experience Southern hospitality and food at Warmdaddy's, not to mention jazz, blues, and R&B music. There's live entertainment every night—from nationally known artists to rising stars and including a comedy night and open jam session.

Other standouts include Time Restaurant with live jazz, funk, and soul nightly in a posh sixty-seat dining room with a bar; weekend jazz at Paris Wine Bar, a charming French-inspired bistro owned by longtime Philadelphia restaurateurs Terry Berch McNally and Chef Michael McNally; Heritage, a hip, homey jazz bar with several dozen beers on draft; and South, a newbie serving Southern fare and owned by the Bynum Brothers, who are experts in both dining and jazz.

TIP
For a memorable day, visit the Philadelphia Museum of Art then walk to Fairmount for dinner at La Calaca Feliz followed by jazz and wine on draft at Paris Wine Bar.

Chris' Jazz Cafe (Avenue of the Arts)
1421 Sansom Street
215-568-3131
chrisjazzcafe.com

Warmdaddy's (Penn's Landing)
1400 S. Christopher Columbus Boulevard
215-462-2000
warmdaddys.com

Time Restaurant (Midtown Village)
1315 Sansom Street
215-985-4800
timerestaurant.net

Paris Wine Bar (Fairmount)
2301-2303 Fairmount Avenue
215-978-4545
londongrill.com/paris-wine-bar

Heritage (Northern Liberties)
914 N. 2nd Street
215-627-7500
heritage.life

South (Avenue of the Arts)
600 N. Broad Street
215-600-0200
southrestaurant.net

CATCH A FLICK
AT A FILM FESTIVAL

The Philadelphia Film Society's annual Philadelphia Film Festival showcases independent, foreign, and animated movies and short films. The eleven-day festival is held at venues throughout the city.

The eleven-day Philadelphia Asian American Film Festival, the largest Asian American film festival on the East Coast, promotes and explores Asian American and Pacific Islander identity. The Gershman Y's Philadelphia Jewish Film Festival spotlights movies about the Jewish experience, culture, and values. The six-day qFLIX Philadelphia festival highlights American and international lesbian, gay, bisexual, transsexual, and queer independent films. Film buffs will also enjoy the Israeli and Latino Film Festivals, Blackstar Film Festival, Philadelphia Film and Animation Fest, First Glance Film Festival, Terror Film Festival, Women's Film Festival, and Awesome Fest, showing cinema in nontraditional spaces.

filmadelphia.org
phillyasianfilmfest.org
pjff.org

qflixphilly.com
film.org/event-directory/film-festivals/

TIP
In addition to the screenings, many of the festivals hold panel discussions, parties, and other events.

BE ON THE CUTTING EDGE
AT FRINGEARTS

You and Toto will know you're not in Kansas anymore if you go to FringeArts, where you'll see unpredictable dance, theater, and music performances by accomplished and emerging innovators who are pushing artistic boundaries. Prepare to be astounded by performances showing what the voice and body can do at FringeArts's new headquarters in a historic building near the Delaware River, and enjoy its restaurant, La Peg, and beer garden. The contemporary performances stretch the imagination and defy expectations.

During the annual seventeen-day Fringe Festival, FringeArts takes the show on the road with more than one thousand curated performances throughout the city.

140 N. Columbus Boulevard at Race Street (Penn's Landing)
215-413-1318
fringearts.com

TIP
Seating for general admission shows is first come, first served so arrive early. And definitely don't be late because some shows do not allow latecomers. Discounted tickets are available for students and those age twenty-five and under.

HEAR LIVE MUSIC
IN PHILADELPHIA

Vividseats.com named Philadelphia one of the best cities in North America for live music based on factors like the number of concerts and average ticket price, saying the city is particularly good for alternative, blues, jazz, country, and folk, as well as fostering homegrown greats. *Complex* magazine named the Theatre of Living Arts (TLA), the Trocadero Theatre, and the Electric Factory to its list of America's fifty best concert venues. The "Troc" is the only nineteenth-century Victorian theater still in operation in the country and is listed on the National Register of Historic Places.

Other popular places for live music include Johnny Brenda's, a gastropub topped with a concert venue; the Barbary, also known for its dance parties; Boot & Saddle, featuring nearly nightly shows; the Fillmore, designed with great sight lines; Union Transfer, highlighting a variety of music; the Tower, with its great acoustics; and Bob & Barbara's Lounge, home of the citywide special (Pabst Blue Ribbon & a shot of Jim Beam).

TLA (Queen Village)
334 South Street
215-922-1011
livenation.com/venues/14272/
theatre-of-living-arts

Trocadero Theatre (Chinatown)
1003 Arch Street
215-922-6888
thetroc.com

Electric Factory (Callowhill)
421 N. 7th Street
215-627-1332
electricfactory.info

ATTEND FREE CONCERTS
ON RITTENHOUSE SQUARE

The Curtis Institute of Music, one of the world's leading conservatories, sits alongside Rittenhouse Square. The school gives full scholarships for exceptionally talented musicians to prepare for careers as performance artists. Hear the legends of tomorrow— for free—several times a week during the school year. No tickets required. Check website for details. The Church of the Holy Trinity (Rittenhouse Square), just across the square, offers free lunchtime concerts every Wednesday at 12:30 p.m. The one-hour concerts feature local musicians, singers, and Curtis students. The Romanesque church, which is on the National Register of Historic Places, is beautified by stained glass windows and a skylight by Louis Comfort Tiffany.

Curtis Institute of Music
(Rittenhouse Square)
1726 Locust Street
215-893-5252
curtis.edu

Church of the Holy Trinity
(Rittenhouse Square)
1904 Walnut Street
215-567-1267
htrit.org/worship/performing-arts/
concerts-on-the-square/

TIP
Strolling from the Curtis to the church through Rittenhouse Square can be quite entertaining. It's like a human zoo, with fashionably dressed residents, business executives, and young families plus jugglers, street musicians, and much, much more.

ENJOY MUSIC
AL FRESCO

The largest free concert in the country takes place on Benjamin Franklin Parkway on the Fourth of July, as is fitting for America's birthplace. The concert, featuring nationally known talent, is the culminating event of Welcome America, a multiday celebration with festivals, reenactments, and events throughout the city. It's topped off with a massive fireworks show over the Philadelphia Museum of Art.

The Made in America Festival over Labor Day Weekend attracts dozens of top performers and tens of thousands of fans to Benjamin Franklin Parkway for the two-day event featuring multiple stages. Past headliners at the Jay Z–curated event have included Beyoncé, Kanye West, Pharrell Williams, and Nine Inch Nails. Tickets required.

madeinamericafest.com

welcomeamerica.com

Penn's Landing
Columbus Boulevard at
Chestnut Street
215-922-2386
delawareriverwaterfront.org

TIP
Almost every weekend in the summer, concerts, multicultural festivals, fireworks shows, and even outdoor movies are held at the Great Plaza at Penn's Landing. Many of the events are free.

FOLLOW YOUR ANIMAL INSTINCTS
TO THE PHILADELPHIA ZOO

The forty-two-acre Philadelphia Zoo is home to more than 1,300 animals, including many rare and endangered species. It is not only the nation's first zoo, but it has continued to be a pioneer by becoming the first in the world to create a campus-wide network of see-through mesh trails that enable animals to roam. Called Zoo360, the trails allow animals to create their own experiences and visitors to interact with animals on the move.

Other highlights include the two-and-a-half acre Primate Reserve and the Reptile and Amphibian House with its 125 scaly residents. Lions, tigers, and jaguars roam around waterfalls, pools, and plantings in Big Cat Falls, and children learn about energy conservation and barnyard animals at KidZoo U.

3400 W. Girard Avenue (Fairmount Park)
215-243-1100
philadelphiazoo.org

TIP
Ride camels, horses, swan boats, or the Zooballoon, which soars four hundred feet above the zoo for great views of the animals and Center City Philadelphia.

Photo Credit: Irene Levy Baker

SPORTS AND RECREATION

RUN UP
THE ROCKY STEPS

After more than four decades and seven movies, the Rocky steps and statue have become one of the most popular tourist attractions in Philadelphia. ScreenJunkies.com named it the second most famous movie location in the world.

Hum "Gonna Fly Now" as you run up the seventy-two steps of the Philadelphia Museum of Art like Sylvester Stallone did in his Oscar-winning *Rocky* movies. At the top, you'll find that Rocky has big shoes to fill, when you step into the bronze impressions of his feet. From that angle, you'll be able to admire the view of Eakins Oval, Benjamin Franklin Parkway, and City Hall. Then come back down and line up to have your photo taken next to the bigger-than-life statue of Rocky Balboa.

Philadelphia Museum of Art (Logan Square)
2600 Benjamin Franklin Parkway
609-468-4660
rockystatue.com

TIP
If you still have some fight left in you,
book a tour of *Rocky* movie sites or take your own tour.

STROLL PAST
OUTDOOR ART

According to the Smithsonian Institute, Philadelphia has one of the nation's largest collections of outdoor art, in part because, in 1959, it was the first city to establish a Percentage for Art Program requiring developers building on land acquired or assembled by the Philadelphia Redevelopment Authority to dedicate at least 1 percent of total building construction costs to the commissioning of original, site-specific works of art.

One such work is Claes Oldenberg's *Clothespin*. The forty-five-foot steel clothespin dates back to 1976. Some say its clasp resembles the number "76," as in 1776, the year the Declaration of Independence was written in Philadelphia. Others note that it appears to be a profile of a couple kissing, in a nod to Robert Indiana's *Love* sculpture a block away at Love Park and Constantin Brancusi's famous *The Kiss* sculpture at the Philadelphia Museum of Art.

associationforpublicart.org

TIP
To learn more about Philadelphia's large collection of outdoor art, visit the Association for Public Art website, get its app, or take the cell phone audio tour.

Some of Philadelphia's Most Beloved Outdoor Art

Clothespin by Claes Oldenberg (Center City West)
N. 15th Street at Market Street

Dream Garden (Society Hill)
100,000-piece mosaic by Louis Comfort Tiffany based
on painting by Maxfield Parrish
Curtis Center lobby, 601 Walnut Street

Love sculpture by Robert Indiana (Logan Square)
Great places to take selfies or "couple-ies"
JFK Plaza, aka Love Park, northwest of City Hall
and Locust Walk at the University of Pennsylvania

Billy, the goat, by Philadelphian Albert Laessle
(Rittenhouse Square)
Its "brother," called *Penguins*, is at the Philadelphia
Zoo. Laessle's studio was close to the zoo, giving him
easy access to animal models.

Swann Memorial Fountain by Alexander Stirling Calder (Logan Square)
Sculptor's father made William Penn atop City Hall and the sculptor's son made the mobile inside the Philadelphia Museum of Art—all three are in alignment along Benjamin Franklin Parkway.
19th & Logan Square

Paint Torch **by Claes Oldenberg (Avenue of the Arts)**
Tip of fifty-one-foot brush and paint "glob" are illuminated.
Lenfest Plaza at North Broad and Cherry Streets

Bronze Eagle **by August Gaul (Convention Center District)**
Twenty-five-hundred-pound eagle has been there since the early 1900s, outlasting two department stores before Macy's and inspiring the phrase "meet me at the eagle."
Grand Court at Macy's, 1300 Market Street
(Not outside but public art.)

TOUR A
STADIUM

Citizens Bank Park, home of the Philadelphia Phillies, is considered one of the best ballparks in the country. The fan-friendly stadium has natural grass, an open concourse that allows fans to constantly connect with the game, views of the city skyline from the open outfield, and, according to Food Network, some of the best ballpark food in the country, including great vegetarian options. The ninety-minute behind-the-scenes tour is led by well-trained guides full of great stories and trivia.

Tour Lincoln Financial Field, the Philadelphia Eagles' 69,000-plus-seat stadium, which is affectionately called "the Linc." During the sixty- to ninety-minute tour, enthusiastic and knowledgeable guides will take fans to the press box, interview room, suites, and locker room and onto the sidelines of the field. You'll also hear more about the team's commitment to having a "green" stadium, since the Eagles were one of the pioneers of the movement, from using solar panels to composting food waste.

Citizens Bank Park	Lincoln Financial Field
(Sports Complex)	(Sports Complex)
Citizens Bank Way & Pattison Ave.	One Lincoln Financial Field
215-463-1000	Lot K off 11th Street
phillies.com/tours	215-463-5500
	lincolnfinancialfield.com/stadium-tours

GET PUMPED
ABOUT BIG RED PEDAL TOURS

A really fun and environmentally friendly way to see the city is by fifteen-passenger bicycle. Big Red Pedal Tours offers tours of the historic district by day and popular pubs at night. Spend two hours casually pedaling to historical sites, including Independence National Historical Park, Elfreth's Alley, and the Liberty Bell. Or pedal to some of the city's most popular pubs, including Silence Dogood's Tavern, a neighborhood favorite, and McGillin's Olde Ale House, the oldest tavern in the city.

The roofed bicycle has room for twelve pedalers and three non-pedalers. They're happy to pair you with other parties. Age twelve-plus for daytime and twenty-one-plus for nighttime. Wear sneakers or close-toed shoes.

Silence Dogood's Tavern, 216 Market Street (Old City)
215-625-2509
bigredpedaltours.com

TIP
Create a playlist on your phone and your guide will happily plug it into the sound system on the bike to customize your tour.

GET UP AND GO
WITH INDEGO

The city has more than two hundred miles of bike lanes and eighty miles of trails and plans to add more, helping it earn its designation as "One of the Top Biking Cities in the U.S." by *Bicycling* magazine. But there's no need to pack your bike in your suitcase or atop your car. The city of Philadelphia has initiated Indego, a bike-share program. Walk up to any of the one-hundred-plus bike stations, insert your credit card, and ride away with a bicycle. More than one thousand bicycles are available, and each is equipped with a basket and front and rear lights.

Bike stations can be found throughout Center City Philadelphia, from the Delaware River to the Schuylkill, and in South Philadelphia, West Philadelphia (near the University of Pennsylvania and Drexel University), North Philadelphia (near Temple University), and beyond. They're available 24/7 and can be returned to any station, making them quite convenient.

844-4-INDEGO
rideindego.com

TIP
BYOH—bring your own helmet.

EXERCISE WITH LOCALS
ON SCHUYLKILL BANKS

Schuylkill Banks, which runs along the Schuylkill River in Center City, is ideal for bicycling, inline skating, running, and walking. The personality of the urban park is captured in the juxtaposition of the Philadelphia Museum of Art as backdrop for a skateboard park. Watch for drop-in yoga classes and movie screenings too.

Schuylkill Banks is part of the Schuylkill River Trail, which winds from Center City to the suburbs and out to Valley Forge National Historical Park and was named Best Urban Trail by *USA Today*. From South Street, go north up to Kelly Drive and past Boathouse Row. Return via Martin Luther King, Jr. Drive/West River Drive, parts of which are closed to cars on weekends from April through October.

Schuylkill Banks (Fitler Square)
215-222-6030
schuylkillbanks.org

TIP
Access the park via ramp at 25th and Market and Chestnut and South, via steps at Walnut and John F. Kennedy, and at ground level at Locust, Race, and Martin Luther King, Jr. Drive.

Outside Yoga That's Free and Pay as You Wish

Schuylkill Banks (Fitler Square)
25th & Locust Streets
yogaonthebanks.com

Race Street Pier (Penn's Landing)
Race Street & Columbus Boulevard
delawareriverwaterfront.com

Dilworth Park (Center City West)
Broad & Market Streets
ccdparks.org

Whole Foods Rooftop (Bella Vista)
929 South Street
wholefoodsmarket.com

Philadelphia Museum of Art (Logan Square)
2600 Benjamin Franklin Parkway
philamuseum.org

The Oval (Logan Square)
2451 Benjamin Franklin Parkway
theovalphl.org

Bring your own mat, water, and towel.
Check websites for updated schedules.

EXPLORE
FAIRMOUNT PARK

Fairmount Park, the nation's largest urban park, is home to picnic grounds, trails, golf courses, Frisbee golf, and woodlands; the Mann Music Center for the Performing Arts, one of the nation's largest outdoor amphitheaters, with great views of the skyline; Shofuso, the Japanese House and Garden; the Horticultural Center; historic homes dating back to the eighteenth and nineteenth centuries, including Belmont Mansion with its Underground Railroad museum; and Boathouse Row, working boathouses that house social and rowing clubs that are beautifully lit at night, creating one of the city's iconic scenes. The park is especially beautiful in the spring when more than two thousand Japanese cherry trees bloom along Kelly Drive and throughout the park.

One Boathouse Row (Fairmount Park)
215-683-0200
myphillypark.org

TIP
Don't miss the Whispering Benches at the Smith Memorial Arch, a popular first kiss destination. But choose your words carefully because a whisper at one end can be heard at the other.

PUTTER AROUND
AT FRANKLIN SQUARE

Franklin Square is one of the five original parks planned by Philadelphia founder William Penn. It served as a cattle pasture, burial ground, and parade ground for the American military during the War of 1812 before evolving into a park. It's now a great family destination with a classic carousel, playground, and storytelling bench, where you can hear entertaining tales about the park's history; a burger joint with its famous "cake shake," made with Tastykake Butterscotch Krimpets; and miniature golf featuring Philadelphia icons, including the Liberty Bell, Boathouse Row, Elfreth's Alley, Ben Franklin Bridge, and more. The holiday festival has become popular, as have periodic food truck and beer gardens. Check the website for events and seasonal closings.

200 N. 6th Street (Historic District)
215-629-4026
historicphiladelphia.org

TIP
Snap a photo beside the mini–Chinese Friendship Gate on the miniature golf course then take another shot at the real forty-foot-tall Friendship Gate a few blocks away at 10th and Arch Streets.

ROLL ALONG
ON A SEGWAY TOUR

You can cover a lot more ground when you tour the city by Segway, not to mention that it's a lot of fun. Philly by Segway, which starts at the Philly Tour Hub in Old City, offers one- and two-hour tours of the historic sites, as well as a cheesesteak adventure that includes samples of five cheesesteaks, so you can choose your own favorite, and a mural arts tour that features more than twenty murals in Old City, Northern Liberties, and Chinatown. Count on friendly, high-energy guides who emphasize both fun and safety.

Wheel Fun Rentals offers two- and three-hour Segway tours that start at the Independence Visitor Center in the heart of Independence National Historical Park. During the tours, fun, quirky, professional guides regale riders with stories and facts about the city. Bicycle tours are also available.

Philly by Segway by Philly Tour Hub
215-280-3746
phillytourhub.com

Segway Tours by Wheel Fun Rentals
215-523-5827
philadelphia.segwaytoursbywheelfun.com

TIP
Check website for height, weight, and age requirements before booking your tour.

HIKE
AT WISSAHICKON VALLEY PARK

At Wissahickon Valley Park, you'll feel like you're way out in the country, when you're actually sandwiched between the Philadelphia neighborhoods of Manayunk and Chestnut Hill, each a great shopping and dining destination in its own right. The 1,800-acre gorge that is part of Philadelphia's 9,200-plus-acre park system has more than fifty miles of trails. The area—with its forest, meadows, and creek—is ideal for running, jogging, walking, hiking, picnicking, and bicycling. The wide gravel road running through the park is called Forbidden Drive, and driving a car on it is, in fact, forbidden. The wooded area is a favorite for birding and it was named an "important birding area" by the National Audubon Society. There's an Environmental Center, with a green roof, that focuses on environmental education, especially for children.

206 Lincoln Drive (Germantown)
215-247-0417
fow.org

TIP
After burning off those calories, put them back on with a soft-serve ice cream cone at the historic Valley Green Inn.

SKATE ON THICK ICE
AT OUTDOOR RINKS

When you ice skate at the Blue Cross RiverRink, the romantic view of the Ben Franklin Bridge is sure to warm your heart. If that's not enough, you can sit by a fire pit in the rustic but cozy winter garden that's illuminated by thousands of lights or in the warming cottages, where you can get snacks and drinks. Open in the summer too, when it has a "beach shack" atmosphere.

Dilworth Park, on the west side of City Hall, has been renovated and is once again a gathering place, as intended by city founder William Penn. The welcoming space not only is a gateway to public transportation but also has a cafe and activities including happy hours, live music, art installations, and outdoor movies. In the winter there's ice skating, and in the summer there's an interactive fountain that's a real crowd-pleaser.

RiverRink (Penn's Landing)	Dilworth Park (Center City West)
101 S. Christopher Columbus Boulevard	15th & Market Streets
215-925-7465	215-440-5500
riverrink.com	ccdparks.org/dilworth-park

TIP
For uber-romance, rent a private warming cottage at the RiverRink.

Dilworth Park
Photo Credit: Peter Tobia

HAVE A SWEET TIME
AT VALLEY FORGE

Valley Forge National Historical Park was the site of the 1777–78 winter encampment of George Washington's Continental Army during the Revolutionary War, and while it was bitter for the soldiers, it's a sweet place to visit today.

History buffs can take a guided thirty-minute walking tour of the encampment; a two-hour trolley tour including Washington's Headquarters, the Memorial Arch, the Monument to Patriots of African Descent, and other historic structures or a self-guided driving tour. Storytelling benches are popular with families. Entrance to the park is free but there's a fee for some tours.

The 3,500-acre park is also a magnet for bicyclists, hikers, runners, picnickers, and bird watchers. Bicycle rentals are available at the lower visitors center parking area and allow visitors to explore twenty-one miles of trails.

1400 N. Outer Line Drive
King of Prussia
610-783-1099
http://www.nps.gov/vafo/index.htm

TIP
Enhance your run or ride by listening to short audio pieces about the park on your cell phone by calling 484-396-1018.

VISIT THE BUCKET LIST PLACE
FOR BUCKETS, THE PALESTRA

Get tickets for a game at the Palestra, called "the cathedral of college basketball." Since it opened in 1927, the arena has hosted more basketball games than any other stadium in the country, including home games for the Big 5—University of Pennsylvania, Temple University, LaSalle University, Villanova University, and Saint Joseph's University.

The storied venue is the third oldest college basketball arena in the country that's still in use. Maybe one reason for its longevity is that no seat is a bad seat. With only 8,700 seats, you'll feel like you're on top of the action even if you're at the very top of the stadium in the rafters. Located on the Penn campus, the Palestra is also home to the university's wrestling team and the women's basketball and volleyball teams.

223 S. 33rd Street (West Philly)
215-898-4747
pennathletics.com

TIP
Get there early to take a walk around the concourse to learn the history of the Big 5 and Penn basketball.

MARK YOUR CALENDAR
FOR THESE ANNUAL EVENTS

The Penn Relays, the world's oldest track and field meet, is at the University of Pennsylvania's Franklin Field every spring. High school, college, masters, and Olympic athletes from sixty-plus countries compete in 425 races.

The Army-Navy game pits West Point cadets against Annapolis Midshipmen. Pep rallies and competitions are held at Lincoln Financial Field in December.

In June, international professionals compete in the Philadelphia International Cycling Classic, a 12.3-mile circuit throughout the city.

Philadelphia's Schuylkill River is home to more regattas and boat races than any other waterway in the nation, including the Aberdeen Dad Vail Regatta, the largest collegiate regatta in the United States; the Thomas Eakins Head of the Schuylkill Regatta, for seven thousand athletes from high schools through world champions; the Stotesbury Cup Regatta for high schoolers; and the Philadelphia International Dragon Boat Festival.

TIP
For the Cycling Classic, get as close as you can to the Manayunk Wall, a 17 percent grade hill where the race begins and ends.

Penn Relays (West Philly)
215-898-6145
thepennrelays.com

Army-Navy Game (Sports Complex)
phillylovesarmynavy.com
(Returns to Philadelphia in 2017)

Philadelphia International Cycling Classic (Manayunk)
855-PHL-RACE
philadelphiainternationalcyclingclassic.com

Aberdeen Dad Vail Regatta (Fairmount Park)
215-542-1443
dadvail.org

**Thomas Eakins Head of the Schuylkill Regatta
(Fairmount Park)**
hosr.org

Stotesbury Cup Regatta (Fairmount Park)
stotesburycupregatta.com

**Philadelphia International Dragon Boat Festival
(Fairmount Park)**
215-232-7689
philadragonboatfestival.com

HAVE A BALL
AT A PROFESSIONAL GAME

Not many cities have four professional franchises plus men's soccer, or have fans as passionate. Citizens Bank Park, home of the Phillies, has the charm of an old-fashioned stadium with all the modern amenities. The Sixers and Flyers share the Wells Fargo Center, ensuring that from October to April there's basketball or hockey almost nightly. Every Eagles game sells out and there's a ten-year waiting list for season tickets, check StubHub for tickets. The only professional stadium outside the South Philly Sports Complex is the Talen Energy Stadium in Chester, where Major League Soccer's Union play, supported by their rabid fans, the Sons of Ben.

phillies.com
nba.com/sixers
philadelphiaflyers.com
philadelphiaeagles.com
philadelphiaunion.com

XFINITY Live! (Sports Complex)
1100 Pattison Avenue
267-443-6415
xfinitylive.com

TIP
If you can't finagle an invitation to an Eagles tailgate, get into super-fan mode at XFINITY Live! at the South Philly Sports Complex. It has one hundred TVs in six entertainment venues, including the first-in-the-country NBC Sports Arena with a thirty-two-foot-LED HD screen, the largest on the East Coast.

76ers Game
Photo Credit: Courtesy of the Philadelphia 76ers

Liberty Bell and Independence Hall
Photo Credit: Andrea Golod for PHLCVB

CULTURE AND HISTORY

SEE NATION'S BIRTHPLACE
AT INDEPENDENCE NATIONAL HISTORICAL PARK

The nation's most historic square mile, Independence National Historical Park, is home to the Liberty Bell, Independence Hall, Benjamin Franklin Court and Museum (page 97), Congress Hall, Graff House, New Hall Military Museum, and Bishop White House. At least the first three are must-sees.

In 1776, the nation's founding fathers signed the Declaration of Independence at Independence Hall and then returned to pound out the compromises for the US Constitution and sign it. Though it bears the famous crack, the nearby Liberty Bell has become a symbol of liberty for abolitionists, suffragists, civil rights advocates, and others, thanks to its inscription, "Proclaim Liberty throughout the Land unto All the Inhabitants Thereof." Maximize your time in the historic district with a tour by foot, horse and carriage, double-decker bus, trolley, amphibious vehicle, or PHLASH bus, which loops around the city with on/off privileges.

One North Independence Mall (Historic District)
215-965-2305
nps.gov/inde/index.htm

TIP
Get free, timed tickets for Independence Hall at the Independence Visitor Center (March through December).

EXPLORE
THE PENN MUSEUM

The Penn Museum (University of Pennsylvania Museum of Archaeology and Anthropology), which is more than 125 years old, is one of the world's great archaeology and anthropology research museums and one of the largest university museums in the country. The collection, which includes approximately one million objects, illustrates the human story. Highlights include a 3,200-year-old sphinx, Egyptian mummies, some of the world's oldest writing, masks from West Africa, and 4,500-year-old jewelry worn by royalty, much of it from worldwide scientific expeditions sponsored by the museum.

The museum's three floors feature material from the ancient Mediterranean world, Egypt, the ancient Near East, Asia, and Mesoamerica, as well as artifacts from the indigenous peoples of Africa and Native North America.

3260 South Street (West Philly)
215-898-4000
penn.museum

TIP
A docent-led tour, available most days at 1:30 p.m., is a good idea (especially the highlights tour), and it's free with admission.

BE SHOCKED
AT THE MUTTER MUSEUM

The Mutter Museum of the College of Physicians of Philadelphia, which houses medical oddities, anatomical specimens, diseased body parts, and medical instruments, is equally fascinating and disturbing. Start on the lower level, where you'll be greeted by skeletons of a dwarf, a giant, and an average-sized person. Then check out the giant colon and the Chevalier Jackson collection of more than two thousand swallowed objects, including many that will make you cringe; the plaster cast of real-life conjoined twins Chang and Eng, whose autopsy was performed at the museum; and more.

The museum certainly separates the science lovers from the squeamish, and one thing that tips the scales toward "must see" is the museum's sense of humor. The conjoined twin cookie cutter in the kitschy gift shop is a welcome relief after examining slides of Albert Einstein's brain.

19 S. 22nd Street (Rittenhouse Square)
215-560-8564
muttermuseum.org

TIP
For a quieter, if somewhat creepier visit, go on a Monday afternoon when attendance is lighter and groups have departed.

DISAPPEAR
INTO PHILADELPHIA'S MAGIC GARDENS

Lewis Carroll, J. K. Rowling, and L. Frank Baum used words to take readers to incredibly creative alternative universes. Isaiah Zagar uses his art to create an equally unforgettable world. Zagar built an outdoor labyrinth of bicycle parts, handmade tiles, folk art statues, colorful glass bottles, thousands of mirrors, and found objects. Walking up, down, and around his massive outdoor art installation, which takes up half a block, is indeed magical. It's a consuming, three-dimensional piece of public artwork. Mosaics on the walls, ceilings, and floors create a topsy-turvy ambiance akin to Carroll's Wonderland, Baum's Oz, or Rowling's Hogwarts. The indoor gallery houses exhibits of mosaic, folk, and visionary arts. Tours are offered on weekends at 2 p.m.

1020 South Street (Graduate Hospital)
215-733-0390
phillymagicgardens.org

TIP
After visiting the Magic Gardens, walk around the neighborhood, where you'll discover more than five dozen additional mosaics by Zagar on homes and businesses. Guided and self-guided tours of the neighborhood mosaics are available.

BOOK A TOUR
OF THE ROSENBACH MUSEUM

Philip Rosenbach collected fine arts and antiques, and his brother Dr. A. S. W. Rosenbach collected rare books and manuscripts. They decided to start a business based on these passions, and by the time they died in the mid-1900s, they had amassed an astounding collection. Highlights include James Joyce's *Ulysses* manuscript, Lewis Carroll's personal copy of *Alice in Wonderland,* George Washington's letters, and Bram Stoker's notes for *Dracula.*

Half the fun of seeing the collection at the Free Library of Philadelphia's Rosenbach Museum is getting a peek inside the exquisite nineteenth-century townhouse that the brothers shared. It's on one of the city's prettiest streets in one of the city's ritziest neighborhoods and is filled with decorative arts, including furniture, silver, portraits, and sculpture. House tours are available hourly.

2008–2010 Delancey Place (Rittenhouse Square)
215-732-1600
rosenbach.org

TIP
Register for a themed, curator-led, hands-on tour, offered on Fridays and Sundays. Bibliophiles will find the opportunity to handle collection objects a profound experience.

MEET THE STAR
OF THE BETSY ROSS HOUSE

Honor the Stars and Stripes by visiting the home of Betsy Ross, the nation's most famous seamstress. The audio tour of the tiny Georgian townhouse she rented from 1773 to 1786 tells how the widowed seamstress and her seven children lived, gives a feel for the lifestyle of the working class in the eighteenth century, and provides a look at the upholsterer's shop where she sewed the first flag. Interactive historical programming includes an opportunity to meet "Betsy" and discuss women's roles in colonial history.

Changing exhibits rotate throughout the site and in the summer you'll find a Once Upon a Nation storyteller in the courtyard, monthly movies, and more. More historic reenactors and storytellers can be found throughout the historical district, courtesy of Historic Philadelphia.

239 Arch Street (Old City)
215-686-1252
historicphiladelphia.org

TIP
In the summer, if you arrive at 10 a.m. when the gates open, you can participate in the charming flag raising ceremony with Betsy.

STROLL THE
NATION'S OLDEST STREET

There are thirty-two Georgian- and Federal-style homes built between 1720 and 1830 on Elfreth's Alley, the nation's oldest continuously inhabited residential street. Two adjacent homes serve as a museum, while the others are private homes.

Elfreth's Alley residents were not the rich and powerful, but a melting pot of the working class. In the eighteenth century, the tiny cobblestone street was occupied by artisans and craftsmen, many of whom ran businesses from their first floors. Early residents included English colonials, a Jewish merchant, and a former slave restarting life as a free man. During the Industrial Revolution, many German, Irish, and other European immigrants lived there and worked at factories nearby. Visiting gives you a glimpse into the everyday life of working Americans in Philadelphia's early days. Since 1702, more than three thousand people have resided on the street, which is a National Historic Landmark District.

126 Elfreth's Alley (Old City)
215-627-8680
elfrethsalley.org

TIP
To get a glimpse inside the homes, visit on Fete Day in June or Deck the Alley in December.

DIG
LAUREL HILL CEMETERY

Laurel Hill Cemetery, the nation's first cemetery designated as a National Historic Landmark, sits on a hill above the Schuylkill River. The tranquil spot, with architecturally designed paths, tombstones, and mausoleums, opened in 1836. The seventy-eight-acre cemetery is the final resting place of General George Meade and about forty other Civil War–era generals, six *Titanic* passengers, and scores of prominent Philadelphians with last names like Rittenhouse and Strawbridge. A more recent burial is award-winning Phillies sportscaster Harry Kalas, who died in 2009 and whose grave is marked by seats from Veterans Stadium and a large stone microphone.

Take a guided tour to hear unforgettable stories about the "residents" or take a self-guided tour and wander past thousands of elaborately carved marble and granite monuments and enjoy the serene vistas.

3822 Ridge Avenue (East Falls)
215-228-8200
thelaurelhillcemetery.org

TIP
The cemetery welcomes recreational use by joggers, bicyclists, and in-line skaters.

DISCOVER
A NATIONAL TREASURE
AT THE MASONIC TEMPLE

Check out the Masonic Temple, just north of City Hall, which is listed on the National Register of Historic Places. The Masonic Temple took only five years to build, but it took thirty-five years to complete the interior. The cathedral-like building is the headquarters of the Grand Lodge of Pennsylvania, Free and Accepted Masons, and the meeting place of many Philadelphia lodges. Freemasonry is the oldest continuously existing fraternal organization in the world.

The Romanesque and Norman building, which was built in the late 1800s, has seven lodge rooms, which are based on themes of the ancient architectural styles, such as Oriental Hall with Moorish features and Gothic Hall with its pointed arches.

1 N. Broad Street
215-988-1917
pamasonictemple.org

TIP
Movie buffs may recall that the free masons played an integral role in *National Treasure*, a Philadelphia-based movie starring Nicholas Cage.

WITNESS HISTORY
AT MOTHER BETHEL AME CHURCH

Mother Bethel AME Church was founded in 1794 by Reverend Richard Allen, who bought his freedom from slavery. Allen and Absalom Jones were motivated to start their own congregation after being forced to sit in segregated pews at St. George's Methodist Church. Mother Bethel AME is the mother church of the nation's first independent African American denomination. Allen was the first elected and consecrated bishop of the African Methodist Episcopal Church.

The beautiful Romanesque church, the congregation's fourth building, was constructed in 1889. It is a National Historic Landmark that sits upon the oldest parcel of land continuously owned by African Americans in the United States. The church, once a stop on the Underground Railroad, houses the Richard Allen Museum, which explains the history of the AME congregation and houses Allen's tomb.

419 S. 6th Street (Society Hill)
215-925-0616
motherbethel.org

TIP

For a fascinating look at other local sites that played a role in the Underground Railroad, visit Belmont Mansion in Fairmount Park and the Johnson House in Germantown.

CAN YOU TELL ME HOW TO GET,
HOW TO GET TO SESAME PLACE?

Hug Elmo, Big Bird, and friends at the only theme park in the United States based entirely on the award-winning television show *Sesame Street*. The fourteen-acre park located about thirty miles from Philadelphia Center City (downtown) is a must-do for families with young children.

The park has rides designed especially for young children, as well as water attractions, so bring bathing suits and towels. In the newest area, Cookie's Monster Land, children can enjoy five rides, a three-story net climb, and a special soft play area for the littlest tots. Don't miss the Neighborhood Street Party Parade and the chance to see favorite characters at the shows.

100 Sesame Rd
Langhorne
866-GO-4-ELMO
sesameplace.com

TIP
If the clouds don't get swept away on Sesame Street, don't worry. The park's Sunny Day Guarantee states that if it rains continuously for one hour while you're in the park, they will issue a Sunny Day ticket to visit on any operating day during the current operating season.

WATCH LITTLE ONES GROW UP
AT THE PLEASE TOUCH MUSEUM

The Please Touch Museum is filled with interactive exhibits designed to encourage learning through play. The six interactive zones are geared for children ages ten and under, including four areas especially for those under three.

It is interesting to let kids set their own pace and see how much they love doing things that parents consider a chore, like grocery shopping (a perennial favorite), driving carpool, or riding a bus. The museum is all about doing—riding a one-hundred-plus-year-old carousel with lifelike wooden animals, racing boats on a mini–Delaware River, moving trains along a track, exploring the maze in the Alice in Wonderland exhibit, or making bubbles. Make getting there part of the fun by taking SEPTA's 38 bus or a tour bus from Independence National Historical Park.

Memorial Hall (Fairmount Park)
4231 Avenue of the Republic
215-581-3181
pleasetouchmuseum.org

TIP
Rainy days tend to be busy days at the museum. To avoid crowds, visit on a sunny day, on a Monday (which is group free), or in the afternoon.

PLANT YOURSELF
AT LONGWOOD GARDENS

More than one thousand acres of woodlands, gardens, conservatories, and fountains make Longwood Gardens one of the world's premier horticultural showplaces. It's a year-round attraction with twenty outdoor gardens and just as many heated greenhouses showcasing eleven thousand types of plants. Highlights include the Italian Water Garden, the Flower Garden Walk, and the Aquatic Display Gardens. The conservatory is home to exotic flowers ranging from cacti to bonsai and has seasonal displays as well as the most significant fountain collection in North America.

The new Indoor Children's Garden is designed to teach kids about nature and includes seventeen fountains to splash around in and hands-on activities. If you're going to the spectacular holiday show, featuring five hundred thousand twinkling lights and dancing fountain shows, it's a good idea to get tickets in advance on the website.

1001 Longwood Road
Kennett Square
610-388-1000
longwoodgardens.org

TIP
Come to Philadelphia in March to see the Philadelphia Flower Show, the world's oldest and largest indoor flower show.

Eastern State Penitentiary
Photo Credit: Jeff Fusco

HAVE A BALL (AND CHAIN)
AT EASTERN STATE PENITENTIARY

Eastern State Penitentiary was designed based on the Quaker-inspired belief that solitary confinement could reform criminals. The menacing Gothic prison has a church-like interior with vaulted hallways, tall windows, and skylights, perhaps to inspire repentance. Prisoners were in solitary cells arranged in a spoke-like pattern that allowed guards a direct sight line of each cell. It was a working prison from 1829 until 1971 and housed bank robber Willie Sutton, gangster Al Capone, and others behind thirty-foot walls.

In 1994, the endangered site opened for tours. Visitors get an audio tour that leads them through the stabilized ruin and explains the prison's fascinating history. Around Halloween, the prison opens for Terror behind the Walls. Named one of the "scariest places in America" by *People* magazine, it is wet-your-pants scary, with Hollywood-style special effects, costumes, makeup, lighting, and sounds.

2027 Fairmount Avenue (Fairmount)
215-236-3300
easternstate.org

TIP
Don't miss the restored synagogue, underground solitary confinement cells, and rotating art exhibits.

GET TO THE HEART
OF THE FRANKLIN INSTITUTE

Walk through the giant heart at the Franklin Institute and take the Neural Climb in the new exhibit, *Your Brain*. Plan to spend several hours in this hands-on science center, where it's all about learning by doing. Pedal sixty feet across the atrium on the Sky Bike, one of only two in the country, for a new appreciation of gravity, then further your learning at the Fels Planetarium. The popular Sports Zone has twenty-one interactive experiences that show the connection between sports and science. Twelve permanent exhibits, a 180-degree IMAX theater, plus many traveling exhibits appeal to adults as well as children.

222 N. 20th Street at Benjamin Franklin Parkway (Logan Square)
215-448-1200
fi.edu

TIP
Peak time at the museum is 11 a.m. to 2 p.m. Plan to visit the popular heart and sports exhibits either late in the afternoon after schoolchildren on field trips have departed or at lunchtime.

INVENT A REASON
TO VISIT THE BEN FRANKLIN MUSEUM

The Benjamin Franklin Museum is dedicated to the life, times, and legacy of the famous statesman, inventor, revolutionary, diplomat, philosopher, and printer. The museum, which is as entertaining as the man, chronicles his life around five of his characteristics—charm, ambition, motivation, curiosity, and persuasiveness.

Visitors enter via Benjamin Franklin Court, a steel structure showing where his house used to be, then proceed underground into the twenty-thousand-square-foot museum. Franklin reportedly kept pet squirrels, then called "skuggs." Look for figurines of Skuggs the Squirrel with descriptive text throughout the exhibits, which include computer animation, hands-on activities, audio, and interactive displays. Timed tickets are available the day of the tour, but not in advance.

317 Chestnut Street (Old City)
215-965-2305
http://www.nps.gov/inde/planyourvisit/benjaminfranklinmuseum.htm

TIP
Wrap up the tour with a visit to Benjamin Franklin's grave at Christ Church Burial Ground at 5th and Arch. It's considered good luck to toss a penny on the grave of the man who advised, "A penny saved is a penny earned."

SIGN ON TO VISIT
THE NATIONAL CONSTITUTION CENTER

The beauty of the National Constitution Center is that it not only tells the history of the US Constitution, but also explains why it's still relevant after more than two hundred years and how it impacts our daily lives. Start your visit with the seventeen-minute multimedia theater-in-the-round performance "Freedom Rising" and proceed to the high-tech, interactive displays. Take the presidential oath of office on camera, sit at the Supreme Court bench, and head to Signers' Hall to add your name to the Constitution and take selfies with life-sized bronze statues of the Founding Fathers.

525 Arch Street (Historic District)
215-409-6700
constitutioncenter.org

City Tavern (Historic District)
138 S. 2nd Street
215-413-1443
citytavern.com

TIP
Eat like a Founding Father at City Tavern, a reconstructed colonial tavern where wait staff in period costume serve eighteenth-century-style gourmet cuisine. Chef/owner Walter Staib is an Emmy Award–winning TV host, cookbook author, James Beard nominee, and culinary historian.

BE SWEPT AWAY
BY THE BARNES FOUNDATION

With the fortune Dr. Alfred C. Barnes made through his invention of Argyrol, an antiseptic, he amassed one of the world's finest collections of impressionist, postimpressionist, and early modern paintings, as well as African sculptures, masks, and tools; Native American jewelry, textiles, and ceramics; and pieces of decorative art. The Barnes was founded as an educational institution dedicated to promoting the appreciation of fine art and horticulture. The museum's educational method, which was based on experiencing original works of art, continues today through the Barnes-deMazia educational program.

The breathtaking collection holds 181 works by Renoir (the largest Renoir collection in the world), sixty-nine by Cezanne, fifty-nine by Matisse, and much more. The art is symmetrically arranged and paired with objects of art and sculptures, making each wall almost too much to digest at one time—but definitely try.

2025 Benjamin Franklin Parkway (Logan Square)
215-278-7000
barnesfoundation.org

TIP
To thoroughly appreciate the collection, book a tour or use one of the self-guided audio tours.

BOOK A TOUR
OF THE FREE LIBRARY OF PHILADELPHIA

If you think libraries have become obsolete, you've never been to the Free Library of Philadelphia. Book a tour for a brief history of the library, then marvel at the architecture of the majestic Beaux Arts building designed by Julian Abele, the first African American graduate of the architecture program at the University of Pennsylvania, and Horace Trumbauer.

You'll be further amazed by the services offered—cooking classes in a state-of-the-art teaching kitchen, musical scores in the world's largest lending library of orchestral music, authors talking about fiction and nonfiction works, including many *New York Times* bestsellers, and individual tutorials about search engine optimization in the Business, Science and Industry Department. Oh, and they lend books too.

1901 Vine Street at Benjamin Franklin Parkway (Logan Square)
215-686-5322
freelibrary.org

TIP
Save time for a tour of the Rare Book Collection, where you can see such novelties as Charles Dickens's family pet raven, Grip, the inspiration for Edgar Allan Poe's famous poem.

PICTURE YOURSELF
AT THE PHILADELPHIA MUSEUM OF ART

The majestic Greek Revival Philadelphia Museum of Art, the third-largest art museum in the nation, has impressive holdings in Renaissance, American, impressionist, and modern art, as well as eighty period rooms. The collection is especially strong in Philadelphia furniture and silver, Pennsylvania German art, rural Pennsylvania furniture and ceramics, and the paintings of Thomas Eakins. The collection of medieval armor is a kid magnet. Pick up the family guide at the front desk for thought-provoking questions about the collection that will keep children engaged, and check out the year-round family programs, especially the summertime favorite Art Splash.

The art deco Perelman Building across the street gives the museum additional gallery space and room to display its vast costume and textile collection, as well as photographs and contemporary designs.

Philadelphia Museum of Art	Perelman Building
2600 Benjamin Franklin Parkway	Fairmount & Pennsylvania Avenues
(Logan Square)	(Logan Square)
215-763-8100	215-763-8100
philamuseum.org	philamuseum.org

TIP
The first Sunday of every month and every Wednesday from 5 to 8:45 p.m. are pay as you wish.

THINK ABOUT
THE RODIN MUSEUM

This little jewel holds the largest collection of Auguste Rodin sculptures outside of France. As you enter, you'll stroll by *The Thinker* and along a lovely reflection pool and garden with sculptures. The small but fascinating museum is home to more than one hundred bronze, marble, and plaster sculptures by Rodin, including some of his most iconic work—*The Kiss* and *The Gates of Hell,* as well as busts he sculpted as a way of studying the anatomy, facial expressions, and personality of his subjects.

The Rodin Museum offers some real admission deals. It's free to stroll through the lovely garden. For the museum, admission is officially "pay what you wish," though there is a suggested admission price. Or opt for the two-day ticket, which gives you access to the Philadelphia Museum of Art, the Perelman Building, and two historic homes as well as the Rodin Museum.

Benjamin Franklin Parkway & 22nd Street (Logan Square)
215-763-8100
rodinmuseum.org

TIP
Tours are conducted at noon daily, so time your visit accordingly.

· ·

DISCOVER PHILADELPHIA
ALL UNDER ONE ROOF

The Independence Visitor Center in the heart of Independence National Historical Park is the official visitor center of Philadelphia and the surrounding counties. You can get free timed tickets to Independence Hall and purchase tickets to more than one hundred additional attractions. Visitor service representatives can answer questions in nine languages, customize your itinerary, and provide maps and brochures. See free historic movies and enjoy Wi-Fi, snacks, and a gift shop.

Visit the Philly Tour Hub to set up a tour of the city via foot, Segway, or vehicle. The historic building in Old City is ground central for historic tours, as well as the cheesesteak adventure, Italian Market Immersion, Mural Tours, Philly on Tap, Rocky Tours, and even scavenger hunts. Plus you'll find amenities such as restrooms, Wi-Fi, cell phone chargers, refreshments, and even a lounge with televisions in case you need to unwind or catch the score of the game.

Independence Visitor Center
(Historic District)
6th & Market Streets
800-537-7676
PHLVisitorCenter.com

Philly Tour Hub
(Old City)
229 Arch Street
215-280-3746
phillytourhub.com

TOUR
THE PENNSYLVANIA ACADEMY OF THE FINE ARTS

The Pennsylvania Academy of the Fine Arts, the nation's first art museum and school of fine arts, was founded in 1805 by painter and scientist Charles Wilson Peale, sculptor William Rush, and others. The magnificent building on Broad Street, just north of City Hall, houses the art museum and school and opened in 1876. It was designed by Frank Furness and George W. Hewitt and has been designated a National Historic Landmark.

The art collection explores American art from the 1760s to the present day and includes work by Philadelphian Thomas Eakins, who taught at the school, Winslow Homer, and Edmund Tarbell, as well as contemporary artists. It's hung in a chronological and thematic format. The museum shows works by contemporary regional artists as well as students in a highly regarded annual student exhibition.

118–128 N. Broad Street (Avenue of the Arts)
215-972-7600
pafa.org

TIP
Don't miss the Lenfest Plaza next door with the giant illuminated paintbrush (*Paint Torch*) by Claes Oldenberg and Jordan Griska's *Grumman Greenhouse*, a military plane repurposed as a greenhouse.

DISCOVER
A NEW FORM OF ART
ON A MURAL ARTS TOUR

The Mural Arts Program was started in 1984 to eradicate graffiti and is committed to the idea that art ignites change. Thanks to this program, Philadelphia has become the Mural Arts Capital of the World with more than 3,600 delightful, quirky pieces of public art. While it's great fun to stumble upon *trompe l'oeil* murals and portraits, abstracts, and paintings of lush gardens, the best way to see the art and understand how it transforms communities and lives is to take the one-and-a-half- to two-hour Mural Arts Tour via foot, trolley, or train. Tours include information about murals, the artistic process, the artists, and the history of the diverse communities that are home to the murals. Each mural is like an autobiography of its neighborhood, representing something meaningful to its neighbors and artists.

Hamilton Building, 128 N. Broad Street (Avenue of the Arts)
215-925-3633
muralarts.org

TIP
The Mural Mile Program invites exploration of twenty-eight Center City murals via a free, downloadable map.

MELT INTO THE GREAT MELTING POT
AT ETHNIC MUSEUMS

Philadelphia founder William Penn's guarantee of freedom of religion attracted a diverse population and subsequently organizations supporting their traditions and history.

The African American Museum in Philadelphia is the first institution built by a major US city to house and interpret the life and work of African Americans from precolonial times. The American Swedish Historical Museum, the nation's oldest Swedish museum, is dedicated to preserving and promoting Swedish cultural heritage. The National Museum of American Jewish History focuses on the history of Jews in America. The first floor, which is home to Steven Spielberg's first camera, Albert Einstein's pipe, and more, is free. The German Society, founded in 1764 as a relief organization for German immigrants, is the oldest in the country, with a concert series, events, and a library. The new Taller Puertorriqueño El Corazón Cultural Center is the largest Puerto Rican/Latino–based cultural center in the state, with a gallery, performance venue, cafe, and playground.

African American Museum in Philadelphia (Old City)
701 Arch Street
215-574-0380
aampmuseum.org

American Swedish Historical Museum (Airport)
1900 Pattison Avenue
215-389-1776
americanswedish.org

National Museum of American Jewish History (Historic District)
101 South Independence Mall East
215-923-3811
nmajh.org

German Society of Pennsylvania (Callowhill)
611 Spring Garden Street
215-627-2332
germansociety.org

El Corazón Cultural Center (Fairhill)
2600 N. 5th Street
215-426-3311
tallerpr.org

BONE UP ON
THE ACADEMY OF NATURAL SCIENCES

Children, especially, love this museum. The Academy of Natural Sciences of Drexel University started teaching about biodiversity and environmental science long before they were on the public's agenda. You'll find T. rex and other dinosaurs, including the Hadrosaurus foulkii, which was discovered more than 150 years ago in nearby Haddonfield, New Jersey, as well as a variety of live animals, live butterflies in a tropical garden, historic dioramas, and a hands-on discovery center for children. Good luck getting your kids out of the Big Dig, especially after they unearth fossils. This is the place where interest in science can be developed and nurtured. Knowledgeable educators are located throughout the building just waiting for someone to ask them a question so they can share their enthusiasm and invite youngsters to participate in hands-on activities. And don't miss the interesting gift shop, which is full of educational toys and activities.

1900 Benjamin Franklin Parkway (Logan Square)
215-299-1000
ansp.org

TIP
The best time to avoid crowds is after 2 p.m., especially early in the week.

GET ABOARD
AT THE DELAWARE RIVER WATERFRONT

The Travel Channel called Adventure Aquarium, across the Delaware River from Philadelphia in Camden, New Jersey, one of the best aquariums on the East Coast. It's the only place in the country to see a great hammerhead shark and watch hippos, and it has the largest collection of sharks on the East Coast, a forty-foot suspended live shark tunnel, 4-D theater, free shows, and seven "touch" exhibits.

On the Pennsylvania side of the river you'll find Penn's Landing, a venue for concerts, multicultural festivals, fireworks, movies, ice skating, and more, as well as the Independence Seaport Museum. The interactive museum is dedicated to the area's maritime heritage and is home of the submarine USS *Becuna* and the cruiser USS *Olympia*, the oldest steel warship afloat in the world.

Adventure Aquarium
(Penn's Landing)
One Riverside Drive
Camden, NJ
856-365-3300
adventureaquarium.com

Independence Seaport Museum
(Penn's Landing)
211 S. Columbus Boulevard
215-413-8655
phillyseaport.org

Penn's Landing
Columbus Boulevard at Chestnut Street
215-922-2386
delawareriverwaterfront.com

TIP
In the summer, take the RiverLink Ferry from the Great Plaza at Penn's Landing on the Philadelphia side to the aquarium and back.

Adventure Aquarium

DESIGN YOUR DAY
AROUND ARCHITECTURE

The Preservation Alliance for Greater Philadelphia offers architecture walking tours led by enthusiastic volunteers, many of whom are retired architects, who explain the history of different neighborhoods and point out details on buildings you've passed many times before but never noticed. Check its website for dates, themes, and meeting places. No reservations are needed—just show up.

The Center for Architecture, down the block from Reading Terminal Market and across from the Pennsylvania Convention Center, has programs and exhibitions that explain how architecture, urban planning, and design impact daily life. Its Emergence of a Modern Metropolis: Philadelphia tour looks at Philadelphia's many architectural styles and building technologies and details the social, economic, and political forces that shaped the city from the 1860s to the present. Its gift shop stocks hip accessories, architecture books, kitchen gadgets, and more, many created by Philadelphia designers.

Preservation Alliance
215-546-1146
preservationalliance.com

Center for Architecture
(Convention Center District)
1218 Arch Street
215-569-3186
philadelphiacfa.org

TIP
Every October, DesignPhiladelphia explores the world of design with one hundred mostly free events throughout the city.

SPEND FREE TIME
AT THE NATIONAL LIBERTY MUSEUM

The National Liberty Museum, the only museum in the country dedicated to advancing liberty through fostering strong character and civic engagement, has inspiring exhibits about heroes from around the world, including Jackie Robinson, 9/11 first responders, Nelson Mandela, and Malala Yousafzai, the Pakistani student who stood up to the Taliban and received the Liberty Medal in Philadelphia in 2014. The core themes of the museum are leadership and good character, diversity and inclusion, peaceful conflict resolution, and civic engagement.

The museum also showcases works of contemporary art, including Dale Chihuly's twenty-one-foot glass sculpture *Flame of Liberty*. The museum believes glass is a metaphor for liberty because its beauty takes many forms, shapes, and colors; it's strong and durable, yet fragile and breakable; and it allows people to see a reflection of themselves and the world around them in a single view.

321 Chestnut Street (Old City)
215-925-2800
libertymuseum.org

TIP
It's free to visit the interactive exhibits in the Welcome to Liberty gallery.

SEE PHILADELPHIA IN A NEW LIGHT
ON A HIDDEN CITY TOUR

Spent your whole life in Philadelphia and think you've seen it all? If you've never been on one of Hidden City Philadelphia's tours, you haven't. Hidden City strives to stoke people's curiosity about the city and make them fall in love with it by learning about lesser-known, but no less amazing, places.

While most Philadelphia tours focus on the city's colonial heritage, these tours illuminate the nineteenth and twentieth centuries, industry and manufacturing, and the African American history that helped shape the city. The tours are led by authors, archivists, and historians who delve into a range of topics including the city's jazz legacy, its underground transit system, the tombstones in a historic cemetery, and the history and architecture of a progressive church in North Philadelphia.

267-259-7112
hiddencityphila.org

TIP
The best way to book a tour before it sells out is to visit the website and get on the mailing list. You'll also find a wealth of interesting articles about Philadelphia's history.

USE COMMON "CENTS"
AT THE UNITED STATES MINT

Many of the coins in your piggy bank were made in Philadelphia, the largest coin factory in the world. If you see a "P" on the coin, it was minted in the City of Brotherly Love and Sisterly Affection, where coins have been made continuously for more than two hundred years.

It's fascinating to tour the United States Mint, one of only four in the country. The free, self-guided tour takes about forty-five minutes and gives you real appreciation for the history of coin-making and the craftsmanship involved in the design. Get a look at coins actually being made through big windows from forty feet above the factory floor, where one million coins can be made in just thirty minutes.

151 North Independence Mall East (Historic District)
1-800-USA-MINT
215-408-0112
usmint.gov

TIP
Not surprisingly, the United States Mint takes security very seriously. Government-issued identification and a trip through a metal detector are required, and the mint closes if homeland security reaches code orange.

Chestnut Hill
Photo Credit: Wendy Concannon

SHOPPING AND FASHION

STROLL GERMANTOWN AVENUE
IN CHESTNUT HILL

This charming neighborhood was named one of the top urban enclaves in the country by Forbes.com and scored a 91 out of 100 in walkability and is well worth the thirty-minute trip by car or SEPTA regional rail. On the way, you'll get a glimpse of the residents' lovely Victorian mansions. Major attractions include Woodmere Art Museum, with its collection of American art in a nineteenth-century Victorian mansion, and Morris Arboretum, a ninety-two-acre garden with a miniature railroad. Grab an ice cream cone from Bredenbeck's Bakery, a staple since 1889, and stroll Germantown Avenue, Chestnut Hill's vibrant main street. It's populated by independent clothing stores (and chains), home stores, and galleries, plus coffeehouses and restaurants.

7600–8700 blocks of Germantown Avenue (Chestnut Hill)
215-247-6696
chestnuthillpa.com

TIP
The neighborhood, dubbed Philadelphia's Garden District, has a busy schedule of events, from sidewalk sales to the annual Harry Potter Festival, Home & Garden Festival, and an arts festival.

SPEND TIME (AND MONEY)
ON RITTENHOUSE ROW

It would be easy to spend all day shopping around Rittenhouse Square (mainly Chestnut and Walnut Streets from Broad Street to 20th), with its pleasing combination of chains and independent stores. In addition to typical mall shops, you'll find high-end shops by Nicole Miller, Lagos, Barneys Co-Op, and Calypso.

And most interestingly, you'll find fashion-forward independents like Joan Shepp and Knit Wit, which carry high-end designers; two children's stores that encourage grandparents to go wild—Children's Boutique and Born Yesterday; Boyds, with classic, high-end apparel for men and women; and stylish boutiques, including Duke & Winston, Skirt, Shop 65, and Ellelaurie. There are also several beauty product stores thrown into the mix, including Ulta, Sephora, Beans, Blue Mercury, and Kiehl's.

S. Broad Street to 21st Street
Market Street to Spruce Street
rittenhouserow.org

TIP
If your timing is flexible, watch for steep discounts at annual and semiannual sales at Nicole Miller, Lagos, and elsewhere.

SPEND LESS
AT THESE OUTLETS

Love a bargain? Then you'll love the outlets in Center City (downtown) Philadelphia. Century 21 offers 40 to 65 percent off men's, women's, and children's designer clothing, as well as shoes, accessories, purses, and home goods. It can be exhausting to peruse the 100,000-square-foot store, but your tenacity will pay off in savings.

The corner of 17th and Chestnut, just west of City Hall, is bargain-hunting headquarters, with Nordstrom Rack and the Bloomingdale's Outlet catty-corner from each other and the Gap Outlet and Banana Republic nearby. The 22,000-square-foot Bloomingdale's Outlet carries discounted items from the mother store up to 70 percent off retail, as well as items unique to the outlet. You'll find Nordstrom merchandise at 30 to 70 percent off at Nordstrom Rack's three-story, 39,000-square-foot store.

TIP
With no sales tax on clothing and shoes, you'll be saving even more money in Philadelphia.

Century 21 (Convention Center District)
821 Market Street
215-952-2121
c21stores.com

Bloomingdale's Outlet (Rittenhouse Square)
Liberty Place, 1625 Chestnut Street
267-858-3200
locations.bloomingdales.com/liberty-place

Nordstrom Rack (Rittenhouse Square)
1700 Chestnut Street
215-599-6755
shop.nordstrom.com/st/Nordstrom-Rack-Chestnut-Street

Gap Outlet (Rittenhouse Square)
1912 Chestnut Street
215-564-4094
gap.com/products/philadelphia-pa-store-2039.jsp

Banana Republic Outlet (Rittenhouse Square)
1911 Chestnut Street
215-563-4237
bananarepublic.com/products/philadelphia-pa-store-2954.jsp

SHOP 'TIL YOU DROP
AT KING OF PRUSSIA MALL

King of Prussia Mall, about twenty miles northwest of Center City, was already the second-largest mall in the country when it underwent a 155,000-square-foot expansion that increased it to 3 million square feet, adding fifty new dining and retail outlets. It also incorporated modern features like common area dining counters, floor-to-ceiling windows, device charging stations, a concierge-level guest service center, valet services, and more parking.

It now has seven department stores (including Nordstrom, Neiman Marcus, Lord & Taylor, Bloomingdale's, and Macy's) and 450 additional retailers, some high-end and some first-in-market stores (including Jimmy Choo, Diane von Furstenberg, CH Caroline Herrera, Robert Graham, Clarins, Vince, and Stuart Weitzman). Even the in-every-mall stores are special—the Forever 21 is the biggest in Pennsylvania and sure to keep teens busy for hours.

160 N. Gulph Road
King of Prussia
610-265-5727
simon.com/mall/king-of-prussia

TIP
Not surprisingly, weekends are busier than weekdays.

TUNE IN
TO THE QVC STUDIO PARK TOUR

Avid QVC shoppers will be thrilled with QVC's tours, and even if you don't regularly get those distinctive QVC boxes on your doorstep, you'll find the tours interesting. And if you're lucky, you may catch a glimpse of your favorite host or celeb guest.

Enthusiastic guides well versed in the multimedia retailer's history conduct four types of tours, including some that give you a behind-the-scenes look at the state-of-the-art facility and show how the audio, video, graphics, and music are used to create the final package that goes on the air. It's fascinating to see the many sets that look so real on the air, as well as the prop room, green room, and more. Save time to visit the QVC store, with its large selection of QVC's most popular brands and QVC gear.

1200 Wilson Drive
West Chester
800-600-9900
qvc.com/visittour.content.html

TIP
When you reserve tickets, pay attention to rules about what types of shoes are permitted and minimum age limits.

BE HIP
AT THE SOUTH STREET HEADHOUSE DISTRICT

In 1963, the Orlons dubbed South Street "the hippest street in town" in their Top 40 hit "South Street." After all these years, this eclectic street is still awesome, if not for the Orlons' contemporaries, then at least for their grandchildren. Teens, students, and twenty-somethings are attracted by the street's edgy atmosphere. It's full of funky boutiques, tattoo/piercing/body arts salons, sex shops, and other mostly independently owned stores, plus ethnic restaurants, cafes, and bars. The younger generation loves to stroll the blocks, especially on Friday and Saturday nights. Their parents and grandparents may find it an interesting place to people-watch, but they may not fit in unless they're headed to Whole Foods, Serpico restaurant, Jim's Steaks, or Starbucks. Start at Front Street, where the headhouse hosts a farmers market and craft fairs in warmer months, and make your way west.

215-413-3713
southstreet.com

TIP
You may recognize South Street from the opening credits of the TV show *It's Always Sunny in Philadelphia.*

DRINK, EAT, AND SHOP
IN MANAYUNK

Manayunk is a charming historic neighborhood that's a fifteen-minute drive from Center City. The walkable Main Street is filled with appealing Victorian storefronts housing mostly independently owned boutiques selling clothing, art, home décor, and furnishings. Favorites include Spiral Bookcase, which sells new and used books, and Main Street Music, an independent music store. The small town is home to more than thirty restaurants, including many ethnic restaurants and many with outside dining. Jake's, a fine dining restaurant, and the more casual Winnie's Le Bus, both of which have stood the test of time, and their younger, funky neighbor, Taqueria Feliz, are all worth visits. The word "Manayunk" comes from the Lenape Indian word for river, which translates to "the place we go to drink." It's ironic, because Manayunk is also known for its vibrant nightlife and brewpub.

4312 Main Street
215-482-9565
manayunk.com

TIP
Manayunk hosts several annual festivals, including StrEAT Food Festival, featuring food trucks, and its beloved arts festival.

IF THE SHOE FITS...
BUY IT

That's the mantra of Benjamin Lovell, who opened his first eponymous shoe store in 1991. He grew up in the family business, Clarks of England, which was founded by his ancestors in 1825. Lovell's shoe stores carry high-quality shoes that are unique, hard to find, and most importantly, comfortable. That's crucial when you're walking around the fourth most walkable city in the United States (according to WalkScore).

Elena Brennan's Bus Stop is another standout, carrying fashion-forward styles that, before she opened in 2007, were only found in New York, London, Paris, or Rio. Bus Stop was named "Best Shoe Boutique in the Country" by *Footwear Plus* magazine and was mentioned in the *New York Times*'s "36 Hours in Philadelphia." Check out Brennan's handcrafted collection of oxfords. They're made of soft-as-butter leather in gorgeous colors.

Benjamin Lovell	Bus Stop
119 S. 18th Street (Rittenhouse)	727 S. 4th Street (Queen Village)
and elsewhere	215-627-2357
215-564-4655	busstopboutique.com
blshoes.com	

TIP
Splurge! There's no tax on shoes in Philadelphia.

EXPLORE
MIDTOWN VILLAGE

Early in the nineteenth century, Midtown Village was one of the most vital areas of Philadelphia. Later it fell into disrepair. However, in the last decade, it has come back in a big way. It's now one of the city's most vibrant neighborhoods, with more than three dozen restaurants and bars and dozens of boutiques. Midtown Village is also known as the Gayborhood, as evidenced by the rainbow crosswalks and street signs. This unique enclave prides itself on its open-mindedness, diversity, and independently owned and operated businesses.

Stroll into Open House, a funky gift shop, or its sister store, Verde, with chocolates and women's clothing; Bella Turka, for affordable jewelry inspired by designs from Greece and Turkey; Mitchell & Ness, with throwback sportswear; and the other little shops in the neighborhood, until you work up an appetite. Then quench it at some of the trendiest restaurants in town, followed by a nightcap.

From Chestnut to Locust, Broad Street to 13th (Midtown Village)
215-670-4323
midtownvillagephilly.org

TIP
This is where Ben Franklin conducted his famous kite experiment.

CHANNEL YOUR INNER IMELDA MARCOS
AT THE SHOE MUSEUM

Get your fill of shoes without spending a penny at the Shoe Museum at Temple University's School of Podiatric Medicine. The museum is free, but you must make an appointment in advance. You'll walk out astounded by the fascinating history of shoes and fashion after seeing about 250 pairs of shoes from the collection of 900.

This hidden gem showcases a variety of shoes of historical significance from Egyptian burial sandals to Eskimo boots and from the enormous shoes of a circus giant to tiny, cringeworthy Chinese slippers. Also find shoes that belonged to celebrities, including former presidents and first ladies, athletes (Dr. J, Billie Jean King, Joe Frazier, Reggie Jackson, Dawn Staley), and entertainers (Joan Rivers, Ella Fitzgerald, Sally Struthers).

148 N. 8th Street (Chinatown)
215-625-5243
podiatry.temple.edu/about/shoe-museum

TIP
Run, don't walk, to this hidden gem, but do it on a Wednesday or Friday because it's closed other days.

STOCK UP
AT FANTE'S

Whether you're looking for a manual meat grinder and sausage maker like your grandma used, a stovetop pizzelle baker, or cookie cutters shaped like a squirrel and acorn, you'll find them at Fante's Kitchen Shop, a family-owned and -operated cook shop in the heart of Philadelphia's Italian Market. Anyone who loves cooking will enjoy Fante's, which stocks thousands of products, including unique tools, modern equipment, and hard-to-find gadgets. And you can count on personalized service.

The shop was opened in 1906 by Domenico Fante and his son, Luigi Fante, and was run by the entire extended family, including Luigi's three sisters and their spouses. In 1981, the Fantes retired and turned the business over to Mariella Giovannucci Esposito, longtime manager and friend, who now runs the store with her own family.

1006 S. 9th Street (East Passyunk)
215-922-5557
fantes.com

TIP
If you run out of time at the store or don't have time to get there, check out the website for thousands of products.

STROLL THE COBBLESTONE STREETS
IN THE OLD CITY DISTRICT

Paste Magazine named Old City District to its list of "underrated stylish neighborhoods" for its clever street style, unique art scene, and innovative boutiques. Stroll its cobblestone streets and enjoy historic attractions, nightlife, cafes, galleries, and independently owned boutiques selling home furnishings, gifts, antiques, and vintage and thrift clothing, as well as clothing by local and national designers.

Favorites are Vagabond and Third Street Habit, which sell hip women's clothing and accessories; Briar Vintage, offering men's fashions, collectibles, and oddities from the 1800s to the 1960s; My Little Redemption, which carries fresh fashion by Israeli designers; US*US Designer Coop, featuring emerging designers who source and produce in the United States; mother/daughter–owned Scarlett Alley for gifts; and Philadelphia Independents, offering locally made jewelry, purses, and accessories.

Florist to Walnut/Dock Streets and Front to 6th Streets (Old City)
215-592-7929
oldcitydistrict.org

TIP
The first Friday evening of every month, the neighborhood is enlivened with gallery openings and other activities.

GET UNIQUE GIFTS
AT THE FABRIC WORKSHOP AND MUSEUM

Forget souvenir spoons and "all my parents bought me" T-shirts—for memorable souvenirs and gifts, visit the Fabric Workshop and Museum across from the Pennsylvania Convention Center and down the street from the Reading Terminal Market. The Fabric Workshop's museum shop features functional objects like scarves, napkins, ties, and umbrellas—most created on-site—by the notable artists-in-residence of diverse backgrounds.

While you're there, wander into the contemporary art museum, the only institution in the country devoted to creating work in new materials and new media, including sculpture, video, painting, ceramics, and architecture. The permanent collection includes more than 5,600 objects, including significant works by artists such as Louise Bourgeois, Robert Venturi, Denise Scott Brown, and photographer Carrie Mae Weems.

1214 Arch Street (Convention Center District)
215-561-8888
fabricworkshopandmuseum.org

TIP
You can schedule a custom tour to get behind the scenes at the Fabric Workshop and Museum.

BOOK SOME TIME
FOR BOOKS

If you're reading this, you have purchased or borrowed at least one book. Want more? Philadelphia is home to several Barnes and Noble bookstores, including a huge three-story location on Rittenhouse Square with a cafe and author events, as well as a plethora of wonderful independent bookstores.

Joseph Fox Bookshop near Rittenhouse Square has a thoughtfully selected collection, including nonfiction, literary fiction, architecture, art, poetry, and children's books. It's the official bookseller for author events at the Free Library of Philadelphia. Giovanni's Room is the nation's oldest LGBT bookstore. Suburban standouts like Main Point Books, Children's Book World, and Open Book Bookstore are great matchmakers, helping readers make the perfect selection.

TIP
The Free Library of Philadelphia hosts author talks. If you miss your favorite, podcasts are available on its website.

Joseph Fox Bookshop (Rittenhouse Square)
1724 Sansom Street
215-563-4184
foxbookshop.com

Main Point Books
116 North Wayne Avenue, Wayne
610-525-1480
mainpointbooks.com

Children's Book World
17 Haverford Station Road, Haverford
610-642-6274
childrensbookworld.net

Open Book Bookstore
7900 High School Road, Elkins Park
267-627-4888
lynnrosen.com/bookstore

Giovanni's Room (Midtown Village)
345 S. 12th Street
215-923-2960
phillyaidsthriftatgiovannisroom.com

BREAK BREAD
AT METROPOLITAN BAKERY

Since 1993, Wendy Smith Born and James Barrett have been titillating tastebuds with homemade breads, pastries, snacks, and granola made with all-natural products, many sustainable and locally sourced from farmers and small producers. Metropolitan promotes other local businesses in the communities it serves, fights homelessness, and supports healthy food programs.

There are now three thriving retail outlets, including Rittenhouse Square with a full cafe, and its products are served at Barbuzzo, Kanella, Vernick Food & Drink, Jose Garces' Volver, and other top restaurants.

For a tasty souvenir you can feel good about, grab a bag of Metropolitan's granola, which was named "best in the United States" by epicurious.com. Also portable are its breads and snacks, which have been featured in *O, The Oprah Magazine, Saveur, Gourmet, Family Circle, Martha Stewart Living* and on NBC's *Today* show.

262 S. 19th Street
(Rittenhouse Square)
215-545-6655
metropolitanbakery.com

12th & Arch Streets
(in Reading Terminal Market)
215-829-9020

4013 Walnut Street (University City)
215-222-1492

TIP
You'll find the recipe for sour cherry sea salt and dark chocolate cookies, and other goodies, on Metropolitan's website.

Metropolitan Bakery
Photo Credit: Rachel Baker

SUGGESTED
ITINERARIES

YOUNG FAMILIES
Sesame Place, 91
Franklin Fountain, 26
Please Touch Museum, 92
Philadelphia Zoo, 53
Franklin Square, 67
Reading Terminal Market, 11
MacMart, 32
Adventure Aquarium, 110
Billy, the goat, in Rittenhouse Square, 58

FAMILIES WITH TEENS
Mutter Museum, 82
South Street Headhouse District, 124
Segway Tours, 68
Franklin Institute, 96
Federal Donuts, 17
Tour a Stadium, 60
Big Red Pedal Tours, 62
Miniature Golf at Franklin Square, 67
Eastern State Penitentiary, 95
United States Mint, 115

DATES

Victor Cafe, 40
Longwood Gardens, 93
Ice Skating at the RiverRink, 70
Terror Film Festival, 48
Capogiro Gelato Artisans, 3
Philadelphia Zoo, 53
One Liberty Observation Deck, 42
Independence Beer Garden, 20
Spruce Street Harbor Park, 20
Hop Sing Laundromat, 7
Love Park, 58

EMPTY NESTERS

Cook, 2
World Cafe Live, 44
Paris Wine Bar, 46
Elfreth's Alley, 87
Preservation Alliance Tours, 112
Mural Arts Tour, 105
Magic Gardens, 84
Di Bruno Bros., 4
Curtis Institute of Music, 51
Vedge, 18

FREE

United States Mint, 115
Independence Hall, 80
Comcast Center, 37
Recitals at Curtis Institute of Music, 51
Shoe Museum, 128
Schuylkill Banks, 64
Valley Forge National Historical Park, 72
Kimmel Center Tours, 36
Fourth of July Concert on Benjamin Franklin Parkway, 52
Rittenhouse Square, 51

HAPPY HOUR/DRINKS

Big Red Pedal Tours Pub Crawl, 62
McGillin's Olde Ale House, 12
Bob & Barbara's Lounge, 50
Hop Sing Laundromat, 7
Chris' Jazz Cafe, 46
Independence Beer Garden, 20
Spruce Street Harbor Park, 20
V Street, 18
Warmdaddy's, 46

NEAR THE PENNSYLVANIA CONVENTION CENTER

Reading Terminal Market, 11
Pennsylvania Academy of the Fine Arts, 104
Center for Architecture, 112
Fabric Workshop and Museum, 131
Hop Sing Laundromat, 7
Chinatown, 6
City Hall, 39
Dilworth Park, 70
Masonic Temple, 89
Miller's Twist, 22

PHILADELPHIA SITES IN THE MOVIES

Independence National Historical Park, 80—*National Treasure, Shooter, Rocky*
Love Park, 58—*Baby Mama*
Eastern State Penitentiary, 95—*Transformers, Twelve Monkeys*
Franklin Institute, 96—*National Treasure*
Lincoln Financial Field, 60—*Silver Linings Playbook*
Boathouse Row, 66—*The Sixth Sense*
City Hall, 39—*Philadelphia, Blowout*
Curtis Institute of Music, 51—*Trading Places*
Geno's Steaks, 23—*Fallen*
Pat's King of Steaks, 23—*Invincible, Rocky*
Italian Market, 19—*In Her Shoes, Rocky*

ACTIVITIES
BY SEASON

While some activities can be enjoyed year-round, others are best during certain times of year. Here's a quick and handy guide to the best seasonal activities.

SPRING

Laurel Hill Cemetery, 88
Longwood Gardens, 93
Indego, 63
Valley Forge National Historical Park, 72
Capogiro Gelato Artisans, 3
Italian Market, 19
Fairmount Park, 66
Manayunk, 125
Rittenhouse Square, 51

SUMMER

Spruce Street Harbor Park, 20
Independence Beer Garden, 20
Eastern State Penitentiary, 95
Rodin Museum, 102
Franklin Fountain, 26
Sesame Place, 91
Wissahickon Valley Park, 69
First Friday in Old City, 130
Franklin Square, 67
Outside Yoga, 65

FALL

WINTER

Longwood Gardens
Photo Credit: Harold Davis

INDEX

One Liberty Observation Deck
Photo Credit: Irene Levy Baker